# JULIA NEWBERRY'S
## Diary

*Julia K. Newberry.*

# JULIA
# NEWBERRY'S
# Diary

## WITH AN INTRODUCTION BY

### MARGARET AYER BARNES

### AND

### JANET AYER FAIRBANK

## W. W. NORTON & CO., INC.
### NEW YORK

# INTRODUCTION

CHICAGO *is so young a city that a hundred years spans its history. In the early years of the 19th Century it was no more than a collection of log cabins, built stragglingly along the shores of its Y-shaped river, within a stone's throw of the protecting block house of Fort Dearborn. Grandparents of Chicagoans living to-day ran for refuge from the Indians behind that stout stockade. Its tiny enclosure sufficed to shelter the entire population of the village that has now grown to house three million five hundred thousand people. In the memory of men and women living to-day the city streets were cut through the encircling prairie.*

*The story of its development is a fairy tale, a saga of the enterprise of the American frontiersman. It occurred in a rich land of opportunity and rapid material expansion, where busi-*

▼

*ness flourished like the proverbial green bay tree and fortunes were quickly made. It is not, however, in the making of those fortunes but in the spending of them that the interest of the Chicago antiquarian centers.*

*It is difficult for anyone not born a Chicagoan to believe that the city of even the late Sixties or early Seventies could have been anything more than a frontier town, a trading post on the edge of the wilderness, but on the contrary, it was a place where delightful people lived with elegance, in close touch with the culture and civilization of the Atlantic seaboard, from which many of them had lately come. Its citizens were occupied not only with the industrial development of Chicago, but were interested in things of the mind and of the spirit. They established comfortable, even luxurious homes, they sent their sons to Eastern colleges and their daughters to Eastern finishing schools. They found time to read, to buy pic-*

*tures, to sit for their portraits to the artists of the period. Their touch with the world at large was astonishingly wide. Their wives and daughters also read and sat for their portraits as well —in Worth gowns, imported from Paris. They sketched and painted in water colour, and played the piano-forte and drove out in their open barouches through the city parks, under tiny, tip-tilted parasols, just as the ladies were doing one thousand miles east of them.*

*To all old Chicagoans this is a twice told tale. The miracle of its truth is lost in familiarity. Grandfather's Healy portrait, grandmother's Lowestoft tea set, father's first editions of Thackeray or bound volumes of Punch, mother's seed pearl brooch and earrings which were the gift of the groom, are possessions accepted as a matter of course and handed down from father to son, or from mother to daughter, in the casual course of the succeeding generations.*

*These heirlooms are rare, merely because of the wholesale destruction of the Chicago Fire, which occurred in 1871, only thirty-eight years after the city's incorporation as a town. No one other than a Chicagoan could believe that there existed, at that time, so much of cultural significance to be destroyed, or could realize that in the imperial song of the city's material expansion, the thud of picks on prairie and the ring of hammer on nails, there can be heard at such an early date the grace notes of a leisurely and cultured life. The story of this fabulous past has been handed down mainly by word of mouth, for the early Chicagoans, although appreciative of artistic expression, were not themselves creative artists. They rarely committed their impressions to paper and bound them in book form. Few formal records remain, for letters, diaries, journals and personal documents of all kinds were burned in the great fire of 1871.*

*This fact gives great value to the diary of Julia Newberry, which we have the honour to introduce to its modern public. It is a journal of two years of a young girl's life, a young girl whose roots were so deeply imbedded in Chicago soil, that though the diary quickly takes us from the familiar background of what all older Chicagoans remember as "the Newberry lot" to the more exploited one of Europe, the reader keeps with its young author a wistful nostalgia for Chicago scenes. Wherever she is and whatever she does she remains proudly a Chicagoan, and Chicago, itself, may be proud to recognize in her, in temperament and expression, a descriptive artist. She says on May 9th, 1870, on the eve of her final trip to Europe; "It nearlly breaks my heart to think of leaving it all & going to Europe again, & I am so afraid I shall get to be like every-one else, & not want to come home, getting so accustomed to the life over there, that I shall care for nothing else.*

I like Chicago so much, so much better than any other place, & we have such a beautiful home, & it is all associated with Papa, & now to go & leave it all! If I only keep on liking it just as well, why then when I am an old maid I can always live here, & even if I should marry, My husband will have to live here, & there is one comfort in that, for then my children would live here too, & it would all go down in the family."

Her father and mother, Walter L. and Julia Butler Newberry, were among the youthful city's most distinguished citizens. The girlhood friends of whom she writes in the journal's pages are the parents and grandparents of the men and women who to-day are carrying on the best traditions of the city's life. An important public library in Chicago bears the Newberry name and was founded through the ultimate disposition of the family fortune.

The diary not only recreates the life of the city with extraordinary fidelity, but it presents *an unforgettable portrait of a young girl. It is written with simplicity, humor and an extraordinary lack of self-consciousness. In its pages Julia Newberry in criticizing "Lucy Howard's Journal," which she read in book form, says; "She had evidently a great deal of book-knowledge, but seems lacking in what young girls almost always possess, namely, fun, humour, sarcasm & enthusiasm." These qualities are essentially Julia Newberry's own and her story is told with a felicity of phrase and an accuracy of observation which is almost incredible in a young girl of from fifteen to seventeen years. The diary reads like a novelist's note book and it is possible that the untimely death of Julia Newberry may have deprived Chicago of a Victorian writer of fiction: undoubtedly it deprived her intimate circle of a spirited, witty and trenchant critic of her little world.*

*Even in Europe she preserved her native independence. She was never dazzled by the so-*

phisticated society there, in which her mother
moved. In 1870 she says of General Sheridan,
the hero of the recent war; "We had a dashing
call from Gen. Phil. Sheridan the other night;
he is distingué, but frightfully ugly. (perhaps
not frightfully but still anything but handsome.) He is very short, (shorter than I.) very
broad; & his eyes are only long narrow holes.
His head . . . is sunk between his shoulders &
his mouth is covered with a large moustache.
He has a nice foot, & good manners, an irish
accent, & when any-one makes a common-place
remark or says something that does not interest
him, he says, 'um, um, yes, yes,' in the most
aggravating manner. He has a good deal of the
'General' about him, though he is very modest, & well-bred; he is very complimentary to
ladies, & evidently is a great admirer of female
beauty. He made me a great many sweet
speeches, none of which were very original."

She gathers from Disraeli's novel, "Lo-

*thaire" that it is "trash" and that "his plebian adoration of the English Aristocracy is disgusting." When she first heard and saw Johann Strauss, she said he "acted like a monkey," but on another occasion she describes a ball in Baden in these terms; "When Strauss led it was perfectly magnificent; he inspires the band to such a degree, that they play as if under enchantment; . . . Strauss is beyond anything I ever imagined; we got so excited, that Mamie & I nearly screamed, & she kept squeezing my hand & 'oh Julia it is too beautiful, I must dance! I cant keep still.'—Even Sister who is so cold-blooded & never gets wrought up by anything of the kind, was wildly excited; & when the cotillon began & he led the first waltz, I thought we should go crazy; I never, never heard anything so beautiful. . . . We went home in a rapturous state, after a never to be forgotten evening, & my brain played waltz after waltz all night long."*

*Her impressions of less distinguished people are no less amusing, and it is in them that we see the potential novelist at her best. The endearing and provoking peculiarities of her father and mother, of her sister's beaux and her own, of the girls she knew, at home, in boarding school and abroad, are all touched off for us with the insight and the terse economy of words which we have come to believe characteristic of the modern writer. "Mr. Little never paid compliments, but he did complimentary things." "He is very funny and he makes me funny." "He acted just like a woman, in trying to appear indifferent." "He had that charming manner which some men always have towards women, implying that for the moment you are the one person in the world in whom they are supremely interested, & a kind of chivalrous deference which is very taking." "I have never enjoyed myself more than I have during the last four weeks. . . . Sister has been fully occu-*

*pied & I always enjoy myself so much more when she is thinking about something else."* *"Sister has a most nasty and disagreeable habit of enquiring when even I get a letter, as to who it is from."* *"I envy people who believe in dreams, visions, ghosts, omens and presentiments, it must afford them so much amusement."* *"I have been reading Wordsworth, & trying to like him, but I dont! . . . But Coleridge's Ancient Mariner is simply superb, & it gives me the same uneasy feeling that Poe's Raven does."* *"I dont believe that I shall ever be in love!—I do not believe that every one is capable of feeling a high, pure, disinterested affection. I believe a certain number of people are capable of feeling it; that a small number do feel, & that a very, very small number of people are loved in return in an equal degree. Therefor, as the number is so exceedingly small, it is highly improbable that I shall be an exception to the general rule."* *"If I were obliged to earn*

*my living I might make a name for myself that
will last, but situated as I am, it is more than
likely that I shall live a comfortable life and die
and be forgotten."*

*Julia Newberry's Diary rescues its author
from the oblivion which she dreaded. She lives
for us again in its unpretentious pages.  Her
period lives with her, but there is nothing dated,
nothing preciously quaint, about her reactions
to life. For the discerning reader, there is in her
work a possible indication that with Julia Newberry a mute, inglorious Jane Austen died.*

MARGARET AYER BARNES
JANET AYER FAIRBANK

Chicago, April 21st, 1933.

# JULIA NEWBERRY'S
## Diary

# JULIA
# NEWBERRY'S
# 𝔇iary

HOME
JUNE 6, 1869
CHICAGO. U. S. A.
IN THE LIBRARY
SUNDAY

UROPE is a dream, Miss Pelets a myth, while hotels, bad eating, & sea-sickness, are things of the past. I know that it wont last but a few months, nevertheless I am home, yes actually at home. Here I am in the old house, where I was born, & where I wish I could always live; it is the dearest place on earth to me, & worth all London Paris & New York put together; Sister & Mother may talk, & say what they like, still I shall persist in my opinion, that there is no place equal to Chicago, & no place like home. It is very diffirent coming home this time, to what our arrival has always been heretofor; very sad, & strange, but *that* is a subject I can not talk, nor write about either.* Our breakfast

*Julia's father had died. at sea six months previously, while sailing to France to join his family.—*Ed.*

3

of pigeons, fried potatoes & corn-bread tasted dili-
ciously, as did also my favorite dinner; roast-beef,
asparagrass, & strawberries. I was made happy this
afternoon by a visit from Annie Tinkham, mercy!
wasn't I glad to see her? she has grown immensely,
& changed considerably; she is not pretty, but she is
very nice looking, and she has very pretty & lady-
like manners. But dear me, she has grown so, & looks
like a young lady. We talked, & talked, about everybody, & everything; I brought her an amythest ring
like mine, with which she was most highly delighted.
We inspected eachother mutually, & with curious
eyes; she wears her hair straight down in curls, which
I don't like. Florence Arnold raced over to enquire
how we were, & she has grown so that I thought it was
Lou Phillips. This morning as I was looking out of
the window, who should I see go by, but Mrs Dodge,
accompanied by a tall & elegant young gent, in light
clothes, & a sky blue neck-tie; & to my utter amazement I recognized him as - - Johny Dodge Esq.
Nene says that he, & Robby Dickey, have been promenading the garden lately, & that both are extremely anxious for "Miss Julia's" arrival; the
snips! Mrs Dickey is very much interested, & hints
about "the children" (Robby & I) having been
"brought up together;" I should think so, when I
have not seen her illustrious son, for four years.

Nene declares that Robby stays over till the 20th instead of going with his Mother on Teusday, entirely on my account; it seems he & Fay, have been flirting pretty well. Nene has fixed the house beautifully; she has a new set of teeth & looks as handsome as possible.

### THURSDAY JUNE 10TH

SISTER has been reading me a story she wrote when she was fourteen, it is too absurd. Fay Calhoun, Julia Rumsey, Minnie Dunlap, Lulu Phillips, Lizzie Whitney, Minnie Whitney & Florence Arnold have all called. They have all grown tremendously.

### SUNDAY JUNE 13

HURRAH! for Mrs Higginson!!! she was down here on Wednesday & paid Mamma a visit. During the call Mother asked her, why when I was in so much trouble, she "my God-Mother" had not written to me? Then it all came out! Mrs Hig. declared that before we went away, Mamma had hinted, (I was then thirteen) that "it would be better if Dudley & I were not to see so much of eachother," that it would not do, etc, etc. And Mrs Hig. like a Motherly hen ruffled up her feathers & said that "of course" she could not write to me under such circumstances," etc. Mamma says she is so proud, that she would rather have her son marry the poorest girl, than

Home

June 6, 1868.

Chicago, Ill. U.S.A.

In the Library. Sunday.

Europe is a dream, Miss Peltz a myth, while hotels, bad eating & sea sickness, are things of the past. There that-it-was! Well—but—a few months nevertheless I am home, yes actually at-home. Here I am in the old

house, where I was born, & where I wish
I could always live; it is the dearest
place on earth to me; worth all
London Paris & New York put together
Sister & Mother may talk, & say what
they like, still I shall never in my
opinion, think that there is no place equal
to Chicago, & no place like home.
It is very different roving home this
time, to what our arrival has always
been heretofore; very sad, & strange, but

FACSIMILE OF THE FIRST PAGE OF JULIA NEWBERRY'S DIARY

"run after" a rich one! Mamma says "she never
thought or mentioned such a thing," she told Mrs
Hig. so, but Mrs Hig. only persisted the more. She
said that "it was very natural that Dudly should
think a great deal of Julia, for he had always known
her, & heard her talked about at home, where they
were all very fond her" etc, etc. And Mamma told
her that she had always thought her boys (she wisely
called them boys) were some of the nicest in town,
& that they must continue to come here (that is Dudley) & that she should be very happy to see them.

CONTINUED JUNE 18

NEVERTHELESS they must have talked to Dudley
about it, for he has not been to see us at all. Annie
Tinkham told him twice that I had arrived, & he
only said "ah! indeed," evidently trying to play
the indiffirent. However the Friday after we arrived
I took an evening walk, & on Dearbon Street who
should I meet but Dudley, & he was anything but
indiffirent then, he wheeled around directly & walked
home with me. He is just exactly the same, I dont
think he has changed a particle or grown a bit, in
fact I dont think he is quite as good looking as he
was; he has the sense to avoid both stove-pipe hats,
& long tailed coats. He walked to the gate but would
not come in (his Father was in the parlor) & it is

fortunate he did not, for Nene told me at the door
that Johny D. was in the parlor. Sister told me not
to go down & see him, but I finally convinced her
that if I saw him that time, then the next time he
called I could be "out", where as if I did not, on
his next visit I should be obliged to see him. So I
brushed my hair, & descended; Johny is now six
feet high & a snip; however he really is not atall

Mamma

Mr Higginson        table        Mrs Dodge

me        Johny

bad looking, his features are very delicate, & his
nose is especially good; when he has a moustache to
cover his upper lip which advances to far, & if he
gets tanned, he will be very good looking if not
handsome. I dont know what his natural abilities
are, but anyway with such a *horrid* Mother, he never
can amount to much. He expects to go to Europe
next Summer after graduating at the Law school.
Sister acts as if I were eighteen she is so afraid of
my seeing any one. That she will never marry I am
morally convinced, fifteen have already sued in
vain, & fifteen more would sue with equal success.
She is an old granny, & rules this establishment with
a rod of iron. Mamma is to be my guardian, & when

I am eighteen her office ceases, & I have entire-con-
trole of my allowance for three years, (or till I
marry, if such an event should happen before I am
twenty-one) & then of course I have my regular in-
come. Stouty & his Mamma sailed in the Ville de
Paris on her return trip, it is perfectly splendid to
have them out of the country, I should think that
that perfect knight (grey haired, & round shoul-
dered), would begin to feel small; I wonder what he
thinks about the "mesalliance" now. Sheffy in my
opinion, is "stark mad", his actions are to say the
least eccentric. In a recent letter, (Sister has refused him over, & over, & over again) he mag-
naimously proposes, to settle his property on his
daughters, & devote his life to amusing & entertaining Sister who he styles "an invalid." Sis. nearly
tore her hair she was so furious. In Paris he worte
Mamma that if we would "only let him come & see
us a little every day in Paris he would *never* mention
the word matrimony", & then he concludes the letter
by saying, that he cant write further for he has "just
cut off the top of his thumb." I have had a visit
from Robby Dickey whom I do not fancy; (I have
not seen him since he was here four year ago, & he
behaved so at Mrs Howes) all the girls chime to
the one everlasting tune, Robby Dickey, & I'm sick
of it. He has very large features indeed, & a thick

complexion, he is a very *good* boy I believe. This morning I received an invitation from Pumpkins to the h. at the Pt. If I was not in mourning I would give anything to go; I was told that he is now exceedingly fine-looking & has a most elegant figure. He does not graduate till next Summer, & if we go abroad, I may not see him for several, or perhaps a good many years; as it is I have not seen him since I was twelve. At any rate if he does not graduate pretty well, I'll have nothing to do with him, thats certain. I sent him this answer.————————

"Miss J. Newberry returns her thanks to Mr ————with many regrets that she cannot accept his polite invitation to the h. at————this Summer."

Mamma made me write it as formally as possible; Mamma is very wide awake, & very much on the alert for such things, she is in fact much more quick sighted then Sister.

### JUNE 30TH
### WEDNESDAY

YESTERDAY the charming Mr Henderson Grant made his appearance, just from New York en route for Omaha. He was most exquisitely put up. *They* took him with *them* to Telie D' Wolf's wedding yes-

terday at five P. M. The bride was pale as death &
trembled excessively, the groom absurdly nervous
& agitated, & the brides-maids seven in number
(Mary Arnold, Telie's Cousin, Mamie Rumsey,
Mary Colts, Molly Clarkson, Mary Drummond, &
Miss Robinson) all looked homely; they were the
plainest brides-maids I ever saw. I thanked fortune
I wasn't in Telie's place; her husband looked hor-
ridly old. Everybody was at the wedding; it was
too funny to see the airs which "the girls" put on
as they came in, & the affected way in which they
sat down. Annie Beckwith in white musline &
Grecian bend, & Annie Douglas looking as if she
were forty. This afternoon Sister & I took Mr Grant
up to Lincoln Park, we had a very jolly ride.

### SATURDAY
### JULY 3, 1869

Lou Phillips came to see me the other evening, she
looked pretty, & intends going to Vassar Colledge
in the Fall, the Whitneys are going too. Fay is going
to Farmington; there will be very few left at home
of the girls next Winter. Mrs Dickey gave us our
Sunday-school lesson at her house the day before
she left. Fay in white alpaca & red trimmings,
Mamie Dater looking very pretty, Lou Phillips,
Julia Rumsey with a chignon, Annie Kelly, & Annie

Beckwith all were there. Robby was of course the
centre of attraction, but he disappointed me in not
being especially sweet on Fay as I expected, which
was strange when it was their last evening together
before seperating for some time; I mischevously
gave him one of the tassels off the fringe of her dress
for a keepsake, for which he doubtless was very
grateful; (or ought to have been). He was *very*
snipish, & is about to enter Yale Colledge, his
Mother of course thinks him perfection.————

This afternoon I saw Amanda Shields driving out
like a young lady; she has grown quite pretty, indeed
all the girls have improved, Fannie Sheldon among
them.

Mamma has decided to reject "the Will" & accept her dower; in accordance with a law, (which
though in existance for twenty years has never been
used, & had been entirely forgotten, & of which Papa
was entirely ignorant,) she will probably have a
life interest in one third of the real estate, & uncon-
trolled possession of one third of the personal estate,
which in our case amounts to over a million. The
affair is to be refered to the supreme court in September. Sister does not like it atall, for she thinks
it will not be doing as Papa would have wished for
he did not know anything about the law, & if he had
he would have made his will diffirently; his main

idea & object was to keep the property so as it would go down undivided to his grand children, & if Mamma should choose to will away to somebody else the three or four hundred thousand dollars of which she will get possession, why then poor Papa's money for which he toiled so hard, will be disposed of in a diffirent way from that which he intended & it seems a sacrilige even to think of it. If Papa had only left us five hundred a year we would never have thought of saying a word, & when Mamma had ten thousand a year it does not seem as if she would have said or done anything. However she does not consider $10,000 sufficient for her support & so rejects the Will. - - C'est drôle. - - - & voilà, tantpis. I wonder if a perfectly satisfactory will was ever made; J'en doute.

SUNDAY
JULY 4. 1869

THERE is nothing like constant occupation to keep people from feeling blasé, the minute I cease doing something I feel disgusted with everything. What a curious thing life is anyway, we are born, then we live, then we die & are completely forgotten; its true the evil that men do lives after them, & the good too I suppose. I dont know anything about my great-grand Mother, & my great grand children *if* I ever have any, will know equally little about me; it makes one feel what a mere atom one is in the Universe. Its a splendid thought for some men to be *"imortalized"*; a reputation that is only to last a few centuries, doesn't amount to much, but to think of Napoleon for instance, or Shakespear who will be known as long as the world exists, & to think of all the unborn millions who will know & admire them, & how in all the ages yet to come, their name & fame will be handed down from one generation to the other; while we poor ordinary mortals, in a few short years will be swallowed up in the great ocean of humanity which has lived, & died. A pleasant prospect truly; its fortunate that the grave is not the goal, & that dust thou art to dust returnest, was not spoken of the soul. If it was, there would n't be much good in living. I wonder if the knowledge that we acquire here, will be useful to us in our futur state? Certainly reading, writing, drawing, painting & playing on the piano wont do us any good; once there was a man who committed suicide because he was tired of buttoning & unbuttoning his clothes; I think it was quite natural, & rather a bright idea of his.—I can understand peoples taking poison, but I cant conceive anyone's being wretched enough to stick a knife into themselves. - - - - -

ANNIE T. spent "the fourth" with me; we painted in the afternoon, & walked round with the girls in the evening. There were quite a number of fireworks, especially at the Nixons. Annie came over yesterday also, stayed to tea & we had a splendid talk. We see eachother nearly every day, & I have taken tea with her twice, since the Tinkhams moved into their new house. They have fixed, & painted Uncle Nich's, & it looks very well indeed. The Tinkhams go East next week, it is too provoking; however we expect to go to Richfield for the sulphur very soon, Sister is not atall well, & needs it very much. I am having a siege with my teeth, & I have to wear a horrid plate, but it is doing them good anyway. I have German three, & French twice a week; I hate German. The other night Annie Beckwith came after Annie & I, with Fay, Lou, & Minnie Whitney, to take a nocturnal ride on the Avenue; we went & it was very jolly. I had a long call from Dudley previous to his departure for the east. (he was going to Evanstone.) Pumpkins has studied so hard, that he has made himself sick, & is now with his Mother on leave of abscence. I had a dashing call from the Douglass's a few days since, in white dresses & black sashes. The other night all of us girls were on the Whitney's step. Annie, Beckwith, Douglas, &

Tinkham, Lou, Nellie Parsons, Julia Rumsey, & Mary Hale, who is quite a young lady, & doesn't attend "childrens parties." Sister & I drove to Lincoln Park last Saturday, there was music, & it was very gay. We are going to add a new dining-room, library, & bed room to the house, with a French roof, & a good deal more; I am so delighted.

### SATURDAY JULY 24

ANNIE Sister & I drove to the park this afternoon, it was excessively hot, & everyone was there. I received a very nice letter from my Shadow, twenty pages long. I am to have a studio over my room in the new French roof, with a private staircase leading to it, & a sky-light; it will be delightful; & what would Mlle Pelet say to the enfant-gâtée now. Every day I thank fortune my stay at Geneva is completed. We expect to get off in a week, & I am to go to Miss Haines this Winter, & so I shall not come back here till Christmas, & then the house will be done. Mr Burling was here fussing over the plan, for three hours tonight. Pumpkins is sick & with his Mother on leave of absence; he studied too hard. Fannie Sheldon & the Sturges's called but I did not see them.- -

Uncle Nich sailed for Europe today.- -

RICHFIELD SPRINGS.
THURSDAY
AUGUST 5 1869.

I HAVE not written for an age, we have been so busy preparing to come here. Annie Tinkham left Chicago last week. The last evening about eight o'clock I went over to bid her good bye, & there of course were the Whitneys, Fay Calhoun, & Charlie Tinkham. We all sat out on the steps, & talked; then Charlie Tinkham went off, & Clarence Burleigh came. We all went in the Library, & then (botheration) came Pussy Jones & Louie Mclagg. And they all stayed for ever, & Annie & I did not have a minute's private conversation, & it was our last evening too. The house was in a dreadful way when we left, & nothing would have induced me to have stayed another week. The workmen had already torn down my piazza, & Mother's bed-room down stairs, every carpet, & all the books & furniture had been transfered to the bowling-alley, & billiard room. It was a most delapidated looking place when we drove off. Ernestine is to sleep in the dining-room to her great horror, for she is in mortal fear of burglars, though Mr Burling has arranged with the police to have the place watched. The last night Mr Isham & Sammy Johnson called. Sammy & I took a moonlight stroll, around the North side;

Sammy was very confidential, not to say affectionate; told me I knew more than half the grown up
young ladies, which I thought was quite overpower-
ing, *for him*. Mr Isham is our lawyer, & very nice
every way, handsome too. We received them in a
bare parlor, even the gas fixtures were gone, & we
had to use candles.

SISTERS BIRTHDAY
AUGUST 12TH. 1869
RICHFIELD SPRINGS

THIS morning Mamma, Sister, Mr Dow & I drove
to Cooperstown, where we remained all day, & then
drove home in the gloaming. We had a very good
time; & had dinner at the Cooper House, & then we
went to see Cooper's grave, in a beautiful cemetary.
Otsego lake is very lovely & only lacks the snow
mountains to make it like a Swiss one. - -. We did
not see the interesting Johnny Dodge but his Mamma
was visible of course.

AUGUST 17, 1869

JULIA DOUW is coming to spend a week with me. Mr
Douw went to Albany on Saturday, carrying my invitation, & sent a telegraph to say he would return
with Julia today. I am very to see if she has changed
in the two years & a half that have elapsed since we
were together in Florida. I wonder if she is pretty,
& as good & prim as ever. Yesterday Sister & I went

fishing, & we caught ninety four fish in all. Fifty-
four Shiners which we threw away, with quantities
of sunfish & perch. Then we trolled, & caught two
pickerel, that is Sister did, & I pulled one nearly
into the boat, & then oh *malheur* it got away. We
had a very good boatman who talked bad grammar
pretty freely.—Coming back I headed the procession & walked into the hotel with this immense string
of fish. Everybody stopped to exclaim & enquire
where we had *bought* them. A lady & gentleman had
sunburned themselves all day & had not caught a
single fish. The first night I came here I was sitting
alone in the parlor wishing I knew the nice looking
girl at our table; when she came in the room, & sat
down by her Mother. "There" said I, "she will stay
there all the evening, & there is no chance of my
knowing her for I would never dare to speak to her
first." I had just settled it, when I saw the young-
lady hop up, & come over to me. So we talked & were
good friends directly. Her name is Bertha Kohlsaat,
& her Father & Mother are German. Here are the
names of some of the people in the house, I'll mark
with a x those I know, & so / those I dont.

| | |
|---|---|
| Mr & Mrs Zebriskie x | not very nice; too many diamonds |
| Mrs Marshal. O. Roberts x. | Nice, exclusive & romantic |
| Miss Roberts.　x N. Y. | Loud, & stares |
| Mrs Crossman.　x | So-so. |
| 2. Miss　　"　　"　　x | twins, & flirty |
| 1. snip　　"　　"　　/ | "Cross" looking. |

| | |
|---|---|
| Miss Bloodgood. / | Homely, sings, is engaged & affected. |
| Mr Denny—. x | Nice - - |
| 2 Miss Dennys. x N. Y. | In the Skinner style precisely |
| 2. Miss Cooks. x | Common, flourishy. |
| { Mr & Mrs Sheldon /<br>Miss Sheldon (forward<br>Polly) /. | Common. Shoddy. |
| Miss Kellog. Utica / | a perpetual flirt of 14. |
| | Young woman with red hair quite a belle |
| Mrs. Lorillard. N. Y. } / | 3 children, 2 maids, one man, 1 coachman. |
| Miss Taylor N. Y. } / | & horses! ahem!!! & governess!!! |
| { Miss Mulford. N. Y. x<br>Pa, & Ma, & brother / | "Beetle crushers, that come down like a thousand of brick." (Mr. Douw) |
| | looks like Conningham. |
| Trowbridge. snip. / | |
| Chester Munroe. nice snip. / | Best snip in the house. |
| Kearney. snip. x | Plays well on the piano. |
| Gould. snip. / | An awful snip we call him "*—" |
| Mrs Pratt. / | Grecian bend. très fort. |

*Word undecipherable—*Ed.*

There are omnibus'es here that go to the woods every little while, they are very convenient when you are bound for the "Lake house", a good place to get boats, potatoes, & lemonade. The music plays for an hour every other morning.

### SEPTEMBER 5. 1869
### SUNDAY

I'M TIRED to death of having company. Julia Douw went home a week ago Friday, Frank & Rosa Kearnan are here now, & Nellie & Meridith Devereux are coming tomorrow! Julia has not changed a bit; she is as good, quiet, & prim as ever, if she does wear trains. But oh! what a strain on the nerves to

entertain her; we had to keep going, morning, noon
& night. There is nothing I hate as much as driving
in the country, & she was very fond of it, & we had
to drive all the time. I know she liked to go sketching but Sister insisted that she didn't & so we had
to go rowing, & bowling, & everything else. Finally
the last day of her stay Mr Henry Pierrepont, with
Jay, & Wittie, drove over to see us from Sharon. We
played croquet. the Pierrepont boys play very well,
& I beat them completely; that was one comfort, but
that we must needs go rowing, & though I was not
well Sister made me go, & I caught a terrible cold,
& was sick in bed for three days. Bertha left the
same day as Julia did, & all the swell people besides.
Mr Bosworth is the queerest specimen; he is a youth,

(at first I thought he was the big-
gest snip I ever laid eyes on)
about twenty three or four, & son
of Judge Bosworth of N. Y. Generally he parts his hair directly
in the middle, & combs it down
very low over his forehead. He
has the very longest nose, & altogether the most comical face I
ever saw. His eyes are good, dark
grey with long lashes & he makes
the most of them. He is very

clever, amusing, & funny, he is over a great deal,
& Mother is rather nervous.—Last night he was over
& we played chess; & quarter past nine I dashed up
stairs to ask my honorable guardians if we could
finish the game; they demeured, & finally decided
that I might have a few minutes more; so we were
just in the middle, when Marie trotted down, with
her horrid, "Madame demande Mademoiselle." &
of course I had to come up. Mamma received an
anonymous letter stating that "a friend wished to
warn Mrs N. against allowing her daughter to receive any attentions from Mr Joseph Bosworth, & he
had openly boasted that he would "secure a rich
wife," & was a thourough fortune hunter." A horrid
impudent letter, & I'm pretty sure the eldest Miss
Cook wrote it, for it sounds just like her; I've been
particularly polite to Mr Bos. ever since, even sup-
posing he is a fortune hunter, how can it concern S.
or I, & I dont believe he is. It seems he & the youngest Miss Gould had a fine flirtation, when they first
came here, & that the families interfered. She is
only seventeen, & is going to Mrs McCauley's next
year. She wears a *very* large chignon, *very* small
waist, *very* short dresses, & is not atall pretty, & how
Mr Bos. could fancy her I cant see, I teazed him
about it last night, & told him that if she had been
very pretty, & without an ounce of brains, I should

have understood it better; and then to save his
vanity I told him I was profoundly anxious, etc,
etc. "Well" he said, "he *really* didn't understand it,
he still thought everything of her, & they had both
enjoyed *it* very much, but he didn't pretend to under-

stand Western people." On my remarking (as I've
done forty times on similar occasions) that I was
Western, he replied "oh! pooh! only by birth;" I
told him he was very rude to talk so about Western
people, when we were all from Chicago, but it did
no good, he insists we are not Western.—Another ab-

surd individual was Laurance Kearney Esq, aged
23. He was forever drumming on the piano, playing
tunes, & whistling; he has some property & lives by
his wits, writing for the newspapers, composing
music etc. Before he was introduced I perceived he
had a tolerable opinion of Mr Kearney, & quite a
ballast of self conceit; so I did not go to work &
admire him as the Crossmans & their set did, & when
he was presented I said how d'i do quietly, & walked
off. After that for a day or two I paid no more attention to him than a fly, & the consequence was he
got to be quite attentive for him, but we had just
become very good friends when he left. He & a little
Miss Wilcox, (soft & foolish) had quite a flirtation,
he used to read alloud "the Gates ajar" to her, both
sitting on the sofa, *very* close together. But he was
a dreadful teaze, for the last evening she was here,
all dressed & wanting to see him in the parlor, he
deliberately put on his hat & coat, & went out to
spend the evening, just to pique her. I told him so,
& he blushed up to the roots of his hair & did not
attempt to deny it. Frank Kernan is a boy, that is
all! he has a great admiration for me, & conse-
quently bothers me to death. Rosa is a very good
girl, but so Motherly, & patronizing, that I am intensely amused the whole time; Sister is pretty well,
though not as much improved as I hoped she would

be. The current story here when we arrived was, that "the Newberrys had arrived, & brought with them, a Greek tutor, a German governess, & a French maid." My going to Miss Haines is fully decided; we go to New York this week for a few days, & then we *shall visit Mrs Osborne at Garrisons*, & I *may* see Pumpkins; we have not met for *three* years, & I'm curious to know if he has changed; & what sort of fellow he is anyway; if he has only got brains, & is clever!

> BREEVORT HOUSE.
> FRIDAY SEPT. 10
> N. Y.

ON MONDAY I drove the Kernans down to Herkimer; where Frank & I took dinner while Rosa talked to Bosworth whom she found down there.—At twelve fifty they left, & at one five the Devereuxs arrived. —Meredith's face is plain but he is very nice & tall, & not atall awkward for a youth of seventeen; he has very nice feet & hands, & excellent manners. Nellie is a very pretty girl; dark with brown eyes & wonderfully heavy lashes; she is nice, & sweet & all that, but there is not much to her. We had a jolly ride up to Richfield, & we were the best of friends before we arrived.—The first evening we played whist, & Meredith & I, beat Sister & Nellie.—Next morning we went to the sulphur spring, Nellie never

drank more than half a glass, but Meredith promised
me, that he would drink as much as I would. So I
forced down each time as much as I could possibly
swallow, & it was great fun to see him take his. We
bowled, once I beat Meredith on a score of 132,
& once he made 203.—, five ten-strikes & two spares
in succesion. We had two delightful rides, one to
Rum Hill, where there is a fine view I believe; we
had ridden about two hours, when I thought I'd ask
the coachman if we were not nearing Rum Hill. And
to our great chagrin we discovered that we had
talked & laughed so much as never to have seen the
view atall, & that we were quite close to Richfield.
—We drove down by the lake House, & climbed to
the top of hill where we had a splendid view of the
lake.—Meredith insisted on lying straight across on
the front seat, with his legs out of the carriage, &
then he entertained us with the most absurd & amusing songs.—The last night some people came over
fom the other house & the Devereuxs were obliged to
dance to make up the set. Mr Bosworth came over,
but I was very fridged indeed, for I was very much
displeased at something he had said.—Then we three
played whist & dragged out our game to the last possible moment, in fact till everyone had gone, for it
was the *last night*. Up stairs Meredith & I had a last
(or rather first) hop-waltz, privately on our own

account, in the hall, & then I went into Nellie's room
a minute. Meredith had previously told me forty
times that he would "do anything in the world for
me," & of course I pooh! poohed the idea. But up
in Nellie's room he said something about smoking.
"Oh dont smoke" said I, "it such a horrid habit."
Well" said he, "if you ask me not to, I wont."—"As
if I would believe all that! you could n't go till tomorrow night without smoking."—"I assure you I
wont smoke till I see you again!" "Do you really
mean it?" "I give you my word of honor that I will
not smoke till I see you in N. Y. which will probably
be a month hence!" "We will see!" "But I promise".
"Still I dont believe you can go so long." "I would
n't do it for any one else but you." "Yes you would
for *Ada Gaffney!*" (a young lady Nellie said he
had been sweet on). "No indeed! she asked me to
give up smoking." "And did you do it?" "No indeed!" "Well we will see!" And now I dont more
than half believe he will do it, though he solomely
assured me he would; eh! bien nous verrons. He
asked me to wish his ring on, & he had a desperate
struggel getting it off his finger, for I could see it
hurt him dreadfully. I wished we might some time
have a splendid long horse-back ride together, &
he wished that I might have a better opinion of him
when I came home from Europe, than I have now.

—Since then I've received a letter from him with his photograph, & he had n't smoked.—The next morning was cold & raw, Meredith & I took our last glass of sulphur water, & about ten A. M. we left, only he & Marie went in the stage. We left the Kitchens smiling on the piazza, the last remnants of Spring House society. We saw the Devereux safely off at Herkimer & ten minutes afterwards left ourselves for New York. We came down very comfortably in a Palace car, the Hudson looked lovely, in the Sunset, our visit to Mrs Osborne is postponed.—

### SUNDAY SEPT 20
### BREEVORT HOUSE

EVER since we arrived, Sister has been better, & I miserable. Sun. & Monday I had an outrageous headache, & on Teusday morn. we went to Stewarts to try on dresses. I stood up a long while, & began to feel very queer, & lo! & behold I had a fainting fit. Such an absurd thing for *me* to do; I felt all the blood leave my face, & Sister who was dreadfully frightened said I turned as green & white as a corpse. For my part I felt most horrid, & decidedly as if I were going to shuffle off this "mortal coil", I could n't have moved to have saved my life.—They gave me water & some other stuff, & fanned & fussed till I was better.—I always wanted to faint once, just to know how it felt; & it is very *nasty;* however hero-ines always faint, but authors never say it is because they are billious. I've been weak as a cat ever since. —We expect to go Garrisons tomorrow. Pump-kins!!!!! I had the awful pleasure of receiving *Miss Haines* & Miss De Janon alone this morning, the rest were out.

Miss H. was *supremely* gracious, & called me "my dear" all the time.—She sat on the sofa & her eyes twinkled; she must have been very pretty; I made several original remarks that seemed to amuse her, immensely.—There is to be a very nice set of girls there this Winter, & I expect I shall like it, & oh I hope to goodness I wont be sickish.

### SUNDAY SEPT 24TH
### BREEVORT HOUSE

WE WENT to Garrisons on Monday, & we had a *pe-culiar* time. The only evening I was in the house, Virginia spent her time in copying a charade, & left me to my own devices. The dinner was rare & costly composed of beefsteaks, & mutton chops. They were tearing down the house, so as to make additions, & we were obliged to hurry off on Wednesday morning to Beverly Cottage, which as we did not fancy par-ticularly, we left by the first train. We had a delight-ful moonlight row on the Hudson, in Mrs Wilsons boat; we must have gone five miles up to old Crow's Nest. Teusday we drove over to West Point, & saw the Parade. There were the two hundred & fifty Cadets, all in a row, all in white pants & grey jackets, & just far enough off to look *exactly* alike. I knew Pumpkins was there, I knew I saw him & he saw me, & yet I could not for my life distinguish him, & among the spectators of course he never thought I might be. It was too provoking; if Mrs Osborne had only had sense enough to have shown us the building where they live, there might have been some chance of meeting. It is three years since I last saw him, & if we go abroad it will be four or five before I see him again, for he graduates in the Spring, & will be ordered off to Vancouvers Island, Alaska, or some other heathen place with his regiment. It is simply abominible.—Tomorrow I expect, (that is if I'm well enough, every one insists I have chills & fever, I think it is fever without chills) to go to Miss Haines, who opened her school last Thursday. *Now* all the girls whom I shall know so well in a month are perfect strangers. There will be nice, pretty, clever girls, & horrid, disagreeable, nasty ones. I never went to a large school before, & I feel the tug of war is coming. I intend to *behave, to like school,* & *not* to be *home-sick,* if anybody can tell me, what more I can do, I shall be obliged to them.

My strong points are Composition, drawing, painting, French, history, dancing, & general information.—I am weak as regards English Grammar, & as I have not touched an Arithmetic for two years I feel uneasy. As to chemistry, astronomy, botany, & natural philosophy, I know next to nothing; this comes from being abroad so much, & travelling all the time. I hav'n't announced the fact, but *privately* I intend to study hard this Winter, & do *something;* that is if I can only have my health. I've made one grand resolution & that is to *hold my tongue*!!!!!! It certainly is a "little member, & kindleth a great fire". "Be somebody, July" Papa always used to say, & "be somebody" I WILL.—I've always been told I had plenty of brains, & every natural advantage; so why shouldn't I be Somebody??? *Laziness* is the bane of my existence.

AT MISS HAINES
MONDAY EVENING
SEPTEMBER 27TH. 1869

ME VOILA enfin! Ever since I was nine years old I've thought of coming here, & now that I am actually at Miss Haines I can hardly believe it. So far I like everything. Mamma & Sister brought me here at three P. M. M. H. then showed us all over the two houses, & I was introduced to all the teachers. I have the spare-room a charming little place. My guardians departed, Marie unpacked my trunk, arranged my things & the dinner-bell rang. I went down stairs, to the dining-room & presently a nice looking girl (Miss Sohier, Boston) came up to me, & introduced me to several other girls. Then in came Miss Haines, who directed me to sit by Miss Leclère the French teacher, in the middle of the table, with Miss Prescott, Boston on the other side. Miss Prescott is a very nice girl; she said she should tell Miss H. she had found a "kindred spirit" & indeed our tastes do agree most wonderfully. She actually likes to write compositions, history is her favorite study, her watch-chain is exactly like mine & came from Paris, & we are just the same heighth.

WEDNESDAY.
BREEVORT HOUSE
OCTOBER 20TH/69

It is nearly a month since I have written, & how much has happened. Oh! dear, for somethings I am certainly most unfortunate; just as I was nicely, comfortably, happily settled at Miss Haines,—I had to leave, - - - & I had only been there two weeks. A week ago last Saturday I came back, as I was feeling miserable, to stay till Monday, but ten days have passed, & I am still here, & likely to be, till January.

—Doctor Metcalf has come every day, & he hasn't decided yet as to what is the matter with me. I'm green, & pale, weak as a cat, I have chills, no appetite, & my head as heavy as lead. To day I'm up, tomorrow I'll be down, one day better, the next worse. I have never been well since I went out that night with the Pierreponts on Schuyler Lake, & caught that terrible cold!!!!—The Doctor announced that it was quite impossible for me to think of going back to school at present, & it is so horrid for I liked it so much.—

### NOVEMBER 1ST
### MONDAY

WE HAVE moved down stairs to day, & we are now on the first floor, in very nice rooms, only they are too much like Paris to suit me. I'm about where I was when I last wrote; I ride nearly every day, but I can not walk a bit, & as I have now been sick two months, I am slightly fatigued. I must now go back to my short stay at Miss Haines. I liked the school ever so much & there were such nice girls. The very nicest were Josie Ludovichie, Sally Sohier, Susie Lawrance, Alice Osborne, Edith Prescott, Mary Williams, Helen Wagstaff, Lolie Buckley, Jessie Perkins, & then there were Saidie Cushing, Miss Nichol, Bessie Powell, May Smith, Jessie Jerome, Frank Lockwood, etc, etc. After some deliberation Miss

Haines put me in the *first* class, where I was the youngest, & nearly all the girls were at least two years older. There was but one morning that I was miserable, & that was when I had to follow the lessons of the 2nd class, & I was so mortally afraid that Miss Haines would make me stay there that I was perfectly miserable; however when it was finally decided that I should stay in the first, we all had a grand time, & I was cheered & congratulated on all sides; it was really very nice to have the girls so glad.—It was very hard, getting up at 6 o'clock, & as I never heard the bell, Jessie Perkins used to come & call me. Prayers & breakfast continued till eight, we walked till nine, when school opened. Miss Leclère's lessons were splendid; I never in either Europe or America saw classes so well drilled; but mercy, we had to have our wits about us. I sat next her at table; several of the girls who had been to Europe spoke French well, but all made more mistakes than I did.—Lessons continued till two when we walked, here were my companions for the Winter.

## WALKS

|  | Morning 8-to-9 | Evening 2 P. M. to 3. |
|------|----------------|------------------------|
| Mon. | Alice Osborne | Susie Lawrance |
| Teus. |  | Susie Lawrance. |
| Wed. | Josie Ludovichie | Edith Prescott. |
| Thurs. |  | Mary Williams. |
| Frid. | Helen Wagstaff. | Lolie Buckley. |
| Sat. | Sallie Sohier. | Sally Sohier. |
| Sun. | Bessie Powell | Sadie Cushing |

From 3 to 4, we could do as we pleased, from 4 to
5, study, & then dinner till half past six when we
studied till 9 or those who wished could go down at
8½ & hear Miss Haines read. "Study hour" was
pretty severe for we could hardly breathe without
Miss Upton's permission, who by the way, was very
nice. We had much reading aloud, & sundry lessons
in elocution from a professor Howe & Miss Mcintosh
a shriveled old-maid, who I trust I may never re-
semble. There were lessons on Chemistry which were
nice, & from which we wrote abstracts,—Miss Oak-
ley was a curious dried up little body, a teacher in
the school for twenty years. The girls were very
jolly, & I got on most swimmingly; by dint of watching my "unruly member" I did not make a single
disparaging remark of either teachers or scholars,
or say a single thing which I might have regreted

while I was there; & mighty glad I am of it now.—I liked it all so much, & I was so comfortable & happy, it seems too hard to have it broken up; & it is so important, I should be there this year.

NOVEMBER 20TH

THE doctor now strongly advises Florida. Sister has written to Dr Bronson to enquire about rooms, & we have nearly decided to go, & take John, Marie, a phaeton, & croquet-box; it will be very pleasant to go to St Augustine again, but I regret school *so* much. Sister left yesterday with the Rumseys for Chicago; she will be gone but a week. I am *very slowly* improving, but I certainly am stronger, & my appetite is much better. Robby Dickey spent last evening with us, it is his Thanksgiving vacation. Lila Moulton came to see me yesterday, we took a drive, & I will confess to you my journal, though to no one else that I was much disappointed in her; she looked pretty & was dressed in the latest style, Tyrolese hat, chatelaine braids, etc. It is three years & a half since we first met; I was twelve years old & liked her very much; since then we have met but once, though we have corresponded most regularly; now that I am nearly sixteen I meet her again; she has nice pretty manners, & I think she is good hearted; but - - - I think she is inclined to flatter, she has a habit of depreciating herself which is affected, & she is decidedly too fond of talking about young men & boys, & she repeated things she had said to them, which were not nice exactly. Mamma never liked my writing to her though she never directly opposed it, & to tell the truth I know nothing of her family, save her Father was a sea Captain, & Mrs Lewis in Chicago is her Aunt. If we go to Europe I shall not see her for years, so I shall be as kind as I may be here, I shall only see her once more, & then, I will gradually (so as not to wound her feelings) leave off writing to her; I'll make a package of her letters, & she will be another of my "decayed friendships"! I'm sorry but I think it will be best to do so. Sister is to be bride's-maid to Ella Low on the 9 of December, who is then to marry Harry Pierrepont; her dress is being made in Paris.—Uncle Nich. is either engaged, or going to be, to a Miss Wolfe, & rich & they say nice young lady here; he acts very queer about it. Capt Tompkins is engaged to Miss Kingsland. Coddy & Sheffy are both in town. Mr Peaboddy is dead, Père Hyacinthe is in America, Napoleon is sick, & Italy has an heir to the throne.— I am reading the 'Illiad', 'Shelly', 'Keats', 'Coleridge', 'Chatterton', 'Héloise et Abélard', "travels in Spain", & painting whenever I have strength. I have had various presents since my sickness; old wine, flowers cut & uncut, cream from the country, pears from Gen. Hooker, horses heads, books etc; people have been very kind. Abott Kinney has been here twice; he has really improved. Johnny Dodge & Mr Bozzy have called repeatedly, but all in vain. —Seth Low is nice, but Jay Pierrepont isn't anything very extraordinary.—Rosy Kearnan has been staying in 37th st; we were very polite to her, invited her to dinner over & over again, & put ourselves out immensely, & She in the end showed herself ill bred, unapreciative, & intensely ignorant of the world; - - * & I were very much miffed at her, & are now. Aunt Butler has been very ill in Oxford.

### WEDNESDAY NOV. 22

THE days roll on, one is just like another. I wake between ten & eleven, feeling dull & heavy, & with a bad taste in my mouth. I put on my dressing gown, & have a little breakfast which I dont relish. I lounge round till one or two, when they make me drive out, bundled up like an Egyptian mummey. We go to the Park & then come home, take our dinner, & go to bed. And oh I am very sick & miserable.—

### MONDAY DEC. 6

LAST Wednesday we had a consultation about me, & Dr Clarke said I had better go to Florida by all

*Word undecipherable—*Ed.*

means. Since it was decided I have felt much better,
& I have now had four comfortable days.—Mamma
went to Utica Friday morning to spend a few days.
—The same afternoon, Mr Bosworth, the two Miss
Litchfields, & Dora Stokes were in, & we made "Plan-
chette" write for the first time.

SATURDAY. DEC. 26 1869

THE Low-Pierrepont wedding came off Thursday,
December 9th & was supremely gorgeous! Mamma
& I arrived early at the church, three interesting
'ushers' in white satin favours assigned us front
seats. Noone but invited guests were admitted, & the
seats were soon filled with what the "papers" would
have called the "élite" of Brooklyn & New York.
Every one was very "swell", & the scene was quite
animated. The organ played a variety of lively
tunes, & finally at one o'clock swelled into a wedding
march, & the bridal procession entered. First came
two "ushers," Gussie Jay & Mr Brevoort, followed
by six groom's-men two-by-two, & then Harry with
his Father. Then the six bride's-maids in pairs,
dressed in alternate pink & white dresses, with over
skirts of "crèpe de chine", looped up "en panier" &
trimmed with morning-glories. Then Mrs Low in
yellow satin & white lace, leaning on her son Seth's
arm, who just at that moment looked as handsome as

a picture; & then came the bride with her Father.
The great Paris "Worth" made her dress, & conse-
quently nothing could be handsomer; white satin
with a long train, & sprays of white orange blossoms
falling all over it, & to crown all a beautiful real
lace veil, made expressly for her. The chancel was
strewed with flowers, & the altar decorated. Coming
back each groom's-man took his bride's-maid as
follows.

| | |
|---|---|
| Hattie Low. | Jay Pierrepont. |
| Miss Jay. | Willie Low. |
| Miss Vinton. | Mr. Constable. |
| Mary Newberry. | Gussie Low. |
| Alice Osborne. | Jay Dubois. |
| Miss Lyman. | Mr Ogden. |

After the ceremony we went over to the house,
where the bridal party were so, arranged.

|   |   |   |
|---|---|---|
| window | | window |
| | Bride & Groom | |
| M. Jay. | M. Low. | me |
| Alice Osborne. | | Sister. |
| Miss Lyman. | | M Vinton |
| people | people | people |

I took Jay P. arm to congratulate the happy pair,
& then I was ensconced in a big chair behind Sister,
where of course I saw everybody & had a most lovely
time. Being excited I had a bright color, & no one,
(Miss Haines encluded) would believe that I was
sick & going to Florida for health. Every one was
so kind, & I enjoyed myself immensely; Jay & Seth
were as devoted as they could be, for acting as ushers they had to attend to every one, fat ladies, old
gentlemen & so forth. I saw any number of youths,
snips, & young-gentlemen; the nicest of those I saw
for the first time were Gussie Jay, Mr Dubois & Mr
Constable, a very handsome young gent. by the way,
a nephew of Mr Pierrepont who introduced him to
me. The collation was "stunning", & the flowers
beautiful. The presents were very handsome, Sisters
was an immense, solid silver fruit bowl, & Mrs Low
said it was the handsomest of all the gifts. Sister's
dress was white, she looked very well, & was much
admired. Mamma went home early, but I stayed with
Sister & saw the bride & groom off to Philadelphia,
where they stayed till the following Monday. Teusday Mrs Pierrepont gave them a reception, & Wednesday they sailed for Europe to be gone a year.—
Thursday evening last I went to my first dinner-
party, & never in my life was I so bored. I had the
illustrious Mr Stuyvesant Fish who in spite of his

having a Grand-Father is little less than an idiot.—
Christmas passed quietly but comfortably, the presents that pleased me most, were a real artist's parasol, from Mamma, & a lovely Madonna in a carved
frame. In the morning Mother & Sister went to
Church, & in the afternoon we drove down to "old
Trinity" where we were decidedly astonished, if not
shocked.—There were about two dozen choristers,
most of them little boys, who were full of mischief.
—Then we chose the opposite end of the town, &
went to see the performance at St Albans, with which
we were soon disgusted. My appetite is much better,
& we made a comfortable dinner, of Green Turtle
soup, trout, grouse, & champagne.—I am glad we
are going away for I am sick & tired of being shut up
here, Dr Metcalfe has been very kind to me & I like
him ever so much, he confidently predicts I shall
soon be well; I am glad for Sister's sake also, for
this hotel life does not agree with her, & she is so
much better now than she was a year ago that I have
great hope that St Augustine will make her entirely
well. And then I can draw & paint, draw & paint,
draw & paint, draw & paint all the time.—

MONDAY EVENING
DECEMBER 27TH. 1869
NEW YORK.
BREVOORT HOUSE

THIS is the last night I shall ever be fifteen; tomorrow I shall be sixteen & when once a person is sixteen, though they are still very young, they can never be called, 'child'.—*Oh Papa, were* YOU *but here!* I am still sick & miserable, & shall have but a dreary birthday, I'm not even well enough to invite a friend to dinner. I have been sick so long, I almost wonder if I shall ever be well; we shall finally leave for Florida next week. I have grown old the last year. I feel it, though the idea may be exagerated by my feeling so blue tonight, perhaps I had better stop writing, for it is nearly mid-night.

> "Trust no futur how e'er pleasant,
> Let the dead past bury it's dead;
> Act, act, in the living present,
> Heart within & God oer head."

DEC 31ST 1869
FRIDAY NIGHT
BREVOORT HOUSE
N. YORK
THE LAST NIGHT OF
THE YEAR

I SPENT my birthday sick in bed: ~~Sister gave me~~
~~$140 in gold to buy a lovely ring like her's in Paris,~~
& one of those lovely painted Madonnas in a carved
case. To make up I went to a "young peoples" party,
at Miss Eliza Jay's last night; we were invited from
"seven till ten". In the dressing-room I found Helen
Wagstaff the only girl I knew there, looking very
pretty in white & pink. We went down together; Miss
Jay is a jolly old maid, who received me very gra-
ciously & then introduced to me a lot of snips;
among them were Mr Hammersly, Mr Sam Howland, Mr Gussie Dubois, Mr Walter Rutherford, &
several more whose names I dont remember. All
were junior members of the "swell" families of New
York; there was a Miss Livingston, & Miss Daisy
Rutherford, who was plain & looked shabby.—etc,
etc. The first quadrille I danced in the back room
with young Dubois; he looked like his brother John
Jay, & seemed very nice. Coming back I saw Seth
Low, & Jay Pierrepont in the hall; Jay had his eye
on me, but he was not going to be in too much of a
hurry, so he talked to his Aunt; (the general as he

calls her) & then made a "bee line" to where I was, &
asked me for the next dance, after which as we were
having one of our jolly talks, Miss Jay approached
& introduced Mr Rutherford, oh such a snip, with
whom I danced the Virginia-reel, though I talked to
Seth Low in the pauses & not to him; Helen was next
to me, so we danced together which was very nice.
Young Howland was now presented he was quite
clever, & as he did not dance we sat through the next
lancers. It was near ten when up comes Jay & asks
me for the next, I accepted in good faith, but when
we reached the other room we found no one knew
how to dance the basket cotillion, & so we talked instead. Jay wished to know if he might have "the
pleasure of escorting me home", I said he might, &
we were very jolly. At ten several people took their
leave, but the rest had no intention of stirring, being
very happy & comfortable; when Jay out of pure
mischief wishing to start them, told the man to play
a march, & of course we had to all go. Jay gave me
his arm, & we sailed out as if he were thirty, & I
twenty at least. As Seth had come with Jay, he came
with us in the carriage, & we had a very jolly ride
home; Marie was there so it was perfectly proper.
They were the two best looking youths there, & I
really liked them quite well. I had a lovely time &
enjoyed the party very much. To think that it is

1870; last year I was at Miss Pelet's, where all the girls have had a great time opening their boxes to night; I wish I could see Minnie.—Many things have happened this year. Uncle Nich is engaged; our house has been rebuilt, Sister is much better, & I have been so sick. Where shall we be a year from to night!

---

12 O'clock, has struck, & the New Year has begun.

---

They are firing the cannon!

---

"The Old year is dying, let him die!"

---

ST AUGUSTINE HOTEL
ST AUGUSTINE FLORIDA
MARCH 16TH

HERE it is the middle of March & I have not written in my journal since New Years Eve; it is a great pity! We left New York January 5, & came via Washington, Richmond (where I was sick a week,) Augusta, Savannah, Jacksonville, & finally Piccolata.—We found a fine new hotel, large clean, comfortable, & with gas in it; rather diffirent from Mrs Gardiners. The house has been full all the time,

some nice people, & a great many horrid ones.—I
can walk a little now, & thank God am much better
than when we came down; I have gained five
pounds, & now weigh as much as I ever did, namely
£132; a pretty good weight for a sick young woman.
The phaeton has been invaluable; Sister has driven
constantly & her dyspepsia is much better;—Mag-
nolia Grove is a lovely spot, & we came in from there
in fifty minutes the other day.—We had some tableaux about a month ago, which were very pretty &
a great success; the proceedes were $800.—Mrs
Edgar at the Florida house got them up, & Sister & I
both appeared in them.—

## PROGRAMME.

### *The Seasons.*

| Spring | Summer, | Autum, | Winter. |
|--------|---------|--------|---------|
| M. Newberry, | Mrs Nesbith, | J. Newberry, | Mr Creary. |

Lallah Rook.

Miss Creary, Miss Reade, & others.—
Good & bad Angel.

Dr Anderson, Miss Gilbert
Lady Jane Grey

Queen
Mrs Roach, Mollie Reade, young Edgar.—
Lady Bright

---

M. Newberry,  Jack Foster,  Mr Creary.
Vintage Scene.

---

Madonna.       Peasants.
Miss Reade, Miss Gilbert, Benidict, J. Newberry, etc.
The Game of Life.

---

Dr Anderson, devil, Mrs Nesbith.—
Night & Morning.
Mrs Nesbith, child, & others.

---

Childe Harold.
Mrs Nesbith, M. Newberry, & some one else.—
Artist's dream.
Leroy Edgar, Mrs Roach, Mollie Reade, Mrs Pell.

---

I enjoyed them immensely; Jack Foster was very
devoted, & we had great fun.—after I came home I
lay awake all night.

List of some of the people that
have been here.

———

Mr & Mrs Glover.
Miss Malbon.
Miss Almy              Boston
Mr Nourse.             snip of 20.
Mr Bremmer
Mr Bennet
Mr & Mrs Sanford. Minister to Belgium.
Mr Crosbie
Mr Shelton             } New York.
Mr Longworth.
Mr Longworth, Jr.
Col. & Mrs Nichols     } Cincinati
Mrs Fred Anderson.
Mrs Aderson.
Gen. & Mrs McKevar. N. Y.
Mrs Wheeler & Mr.
Mr & Mrs Thurber.      } N. Y.
Mr. & Mrs Bracket.  Boston.
Mr, Mrs, & Miss Parsons.
Parsons. Jr. (horrid)  } Flushing.
Kennedy family.  Penn.
Mrs Brede.  Chicago
Mrs Randal. - - -
Mr & Mrs Wiggin    Boston
Mr & Miss Livingston.  N. Y.

Mr, Mrs & the Miss Donaldsons. Hudson River

Mrs & Miss Johnson
snip Johnson. } N. Y.

Mr, Mrs & Miss Holmes
2 snips } N. Y.

Mr & Miss (Kate) Butts. Providence.

Common Mrs Wheeler.

Nice snip Dodge. Boston, did n't know him.

Mrs Ambler ) Jacksonville
Miss Coventry ∫ Utica.

Miss Humphfreys.—Brooklyn.

Mrs Atwater & Mr. N. Y.—

Mrs Bronson
Mrs Hoffman } Ny

Dr & Mrs Dubois
Dr & Mrs Bumstead } N. Y.

Mr & Mrs Ward. Brooklin


I made Jack Foster's acquaintance when I first arrived, but he has been away a good deal. He is very homely, & wears shockingly old fashioned clothes, checked pantaloons for instance.—On the other hand, his blood is blue, his connections splendid, his manners excellent; he is polite, kind, attentive, jolly, amusing, & 23. what is more, he has never said or done anything that jarred me in the least. We had a very nice time together at the tableaux, & he was very attentive. After that I saw

him occasionaly, & about three weeks ago, he made
me a present of a beautiful little alligator, about
eight inches long, & just the right size. When I first
got him, every one announced that he would die; I
said he should-not, we have fed him on raw beef &
he is more lively than ever. I have named him Jack,
& shall take him home.

I had quite an adventure also: I was sketching by
the seawall when Jack F. & his Mother drove by,
& stopped the carriage to speak to me; While we
were talking, my horse gave a jump, & rushed
franticly across the street, where he was obliged to
stop a minute as there was a fence in the way. Jack
rushed after jumped into the phaeton, seized the
reins, & turned towards home; the horse went with
all his might, & Jack could barely hold him in. If he
had not been there, I should have been runaway
with, for of course I could never have managed the
beast.—I rode no more in the phaeton that day; but
I took a ride with Mrs. Foster & her interesting son;
on the way I lost my fur saque, we had a great hunt
for it, & finally Jack met a missonary with it hanging
on his arm.—There have been one or two violent
flirtations; the most amusing is that between Miss
Helen Livingston aged thirty, & Leroy Edgar,
twenty-eight, or a little more. He is tall good looking & conceited, dresses well, & I call him the

Adonis; he lives at the Florida house, Miss Livingston runs after him the whole time, & is evidently far far gone; he on the other hand is excessively indiffirent; There were two Boston girls here, Miss Almy, & Miss Malbon (the greatest born flirt I ever saw.) She was a funny little thing, with pretty little ways, & always wanting a man around. The Longworth party from Cincinati were very nice, especially Mrs Nichols, & her Brother Mr Longworth Jr, a professional artist, who knew music "au fond," spoke four languages, & on top of it all was excessively modest. Then there was Gen. & Mrs Mckivor, of N. Y. The Gen was very attentive, & had the most absurd way of enviting himself to take a ride in the phaeton with me. He would say, "come now Miss Julia, let us take a nice ride this afternoon," & of course I had to let him go; he told me all his love affairs, which were very amusing. I can sketch very well from nature now, which is a great satisfaction; I have done the gates twice, "the fort" three times, St Georges street, the church, the wharf, a small view of the town, some houses, & a tree with moss on it; these are all I have been able so far to do out of doors for it tires me dreadfully. We intend to leave here this week, go up the river to Enterprize, then to New York for a week, arriving home about the middle of April, where we shall stay

till about the tenth of June when Sister wishes to
sail for Europe. I am so unhappy about it, for I
dont want to go abroad again atall, or at least not
till September; but Sister wants to travel in England
& Switzerland during the Summer, & of course we
have to go.—Uncle Nich is to be married in May. I
expected Minnie would have made a grand row
when she heard about it, but all she said is this. "I
was pretty mad at first, but I got over it as I generally do, & hope as Mlle Steiner says, it will be all
for the best." In her last letter Miss Wolfe had just
sent her a gorgeous locket, with Uncle Nich's. picture on one side & her own on the other.—It has
been wretchedly cold here for Florida, & altogether
the Winter has been very diffirent, & not half as nice,
as when we were here three years ago; still I like St
Augustine, & every one does, & generally without
knowing why; one is bored to death half the time,
& yet fascinated with the place; it is so quaint, old,
& diffirent from any other place in America.—My
breath is so short I can hardly get up stairs.—They
had a Presbyterian Fair, also, that was very stupid,
where they made $200. I went to a sewing society at
Mrs Gilberts, & I never was so bored in my life
except at Mrs. Griffins dinner party. Deliver me
from sewing societies!! There is a brother here of
the English Mr Wheeler we knew in Nice, who

looks horrid, just like the Prince of Wales; he has tried every way to be introduced to us, but Sister sails down to dinner, & then sails up stairs, & gives him no chance. There was also a little Mary Kennedy here, that I liked because she looked so very much like Minnie. . . I have seen but little of the Benedicts, for Mary & I, have not one single point in common,

### MONDAY
### MARCH 21ST

THE alligator died last night, a most untimely death, & from no apparent cause; I feel dreadfully about it, & especially so, because I did not paint his picture as I might have done.—The two Fosters came in again last night; I had already bidden Jack good bye twice, when he went out to his farm (twenty-eight miles on the road to Jacksonville) last week. But he decided to come in yesterday morning, on his "calico horse" which for form & color has no *equal* in all Florida.—Mamma, Miss Livingston, & I took a moonlight walk on the sea wall; I did not dare tell Sister, though it did not hurt me a bit.—We went up to the "fort," & then past the Florida where Miss L. was crazy to get a glimpse of her dear Edgar.— All the nice people have left, & the house is full of strange faces, & flashy young ladies. Sister has a frightful cold.

MARCH 22ND. 1870
THURSDAY
LAST NIGHT IN
ST AUGUSTINE

I AM glad to go home, & yet sorry to leave this interesting spot; it is a queer place, & its charm lies in being queer. It will be horrid when they have a railroad, more hotels, & a bridge instead of a Ferry. I suppose I shall see it again some time, because every one comes back. Still it hasn't been nearly as pleasant this year, as it was three years ago, when we had the military, croquet, & fishing. However I shall always be grateful to St Augustine, for being here has saved me from several months, of nasty cold wet weather, shut up in a house in New York.

ENTERPRISE
ON THE ST JOHNS RIVER
FLORIDA
MARCH 25TH 1870

HERE we are in the wilds of Florida surrounded by an impenetrable forest, and a hundred miles at least from any town. Enterprise consists of a single hotel, & one other building; before it lies the river widened into a lake, full of weedes & alligators. The trees along the banks, are all covered with masses of long grey Spanish moss, which produces a curiously weird effect, like that of an "army of phantomes vast & wan." I found a delicious seat this morning, among the roots of a tree, knarled & twisted most fantastically; sitting there, close by the water, listning to the waves as they washed up on the sand, with the feathery palm trees waving above, excluding the heat, & making a delicious coolness, it was indeed like an enchanted forest. We were within six feet of an alligator yesterday; he was floating on the water, green, brown, & hidious; altogether the ugliest creature I ever beheld!

JACKSONVILLE
MARCH 31ST. 1870
THURSDAY

W<small>E</small> LEFT St Augustine Thursday morning in a
North East storm; We had the little stage which just
held us, & Mr Henry (the owner) to drive us over.—
He talked the whole way, & his conversation was to
say the least original. Mamma of course conversed
with him, & drew him out, on every possible subject:

Mamma!—I suppose you make a good deal of
money, driving the stages!

Mr Henry—Wall, yis, we do pritty well, but yi
kant git any one to help yi down here, the niggers is
so lazy, they dont do nothing atall.

M.—You have to help yourself, eh!

Henry—Yes I always did have to shift for myself
pretty much. (to the horses) ge up boys! what do ye
mean sir! Mi father died & left me three brothers
to care for!

Mamma. (Sympathizeingly)
"You dont say so."

Henry. Mi Father was an old
man, but he died just as easy, didn't
mind it any more, than we do going
to Piccolata. He lay in his bed
there,—calm & composed—over
seventy-five people present,—called mi up,—says

Mr. Henry

to me, "Henry take care your brothers,—always stick together! (The conversation grows distressing and Mamma changes the subject.—

Mamma. (blandly). "It is a pity there are no nice cariages in Augustine."

Henry: (to the horses) "(what di ye mean sir.)" yes mam if I could go North, & had plenty of money, I'd git a lot, & bring um down here; I'd go in for style; & get some stylish high teams, with all the appintments, & t'would be a big thing. . I'm trying to get money, & give mi children som iducation; I never had none miself; & I intend they shant be without it, no mam.

Mamma.—"I suppose there are various ways of making money down here."

Henry—"Yes mam! I see lots of chances every day for a man to make money; I made fifty dollars last year out of bottles." (Ge up sir, what do ye mean boys.

All of us.—Bottles!

Henry.—Yes, mam, whenever I seed a bottle lying round, left in the stage, (agents, often drink & leave bottle behind) I picks it up, saves it, & puts it away, end of the season I sell um. Then mum, I saves all the old corn, & wheat bags, & they sell for 8 cents apeice; made ten dollars last month with um. ge up boys, what di ye mean sir! In the Summer

I sell all my old horses, & sometimes keep one or two good ones,

Mam. What is that for!

Henry. Cause I kant afford to feed um; I take um in the interior where they dont know who I be, among the "Crackers"; I tell them, that theer good horses, splindid horses, they believe me & buys um; oh yes mum, there lots a' ways amaking money down here; if a man knows how, & just keeps his eyes wide open.—

Arrived at *Piccolata* we waited two hours in an Equinocial storm for the "Starlight; it poured all the way to Enterprise, where we stayed three days. Mr Charles Butler's family with the hon. Mr Stanley came *down* the river with us, & we had splendid weather. Mr Stanley was a most absurd Englishman, clever, amusing, & very liberal in his ideas. He wore a grey knickerbocker suit, red stockings, & a tyrolese hat. His pistol was the first I ever fired; we saw alligators, blue herons & white cranes. There was a Mrs Ed. O. Rockwood on the boat, to whom Lord Parker was devoted. She was a charming person, & we had a delightful talk.

APRIL 14TH 1870

AT JACKSONVILLE we stayed a day & met several people, Nellie Warren, Boston among others. A night in the sleeping car brought us to the Screven House Savannah. There I found Miss Butts & her Father (Providence) & Mr Arnold. They had a hop there that night, & I went down to look on for a while. I was not edified with either the Southern beauty, or chivalry of which one reads & hears so much. The women powdered, & worse, while all the young men were horribly seedy.—Miss Butts had an admirer, aristocraticly named Jimmy Jones; a young man about twenty-seven. Coming on in the cars to Charleston Miss Butts gave me a detailed account of the whole transaction. How he had first seen her in the street & tried to make her look at him & she wouldn't, & then was introduced on the croquet ground, & he noticed what a "dear little soft white hand she had." She told me with perfect naïveté how he always called her "chèrie" & "dearest", "sweetheart" & I dont know what else. She said he was "such a dear little fellow", & she thought "so much of him", & she "liked him so much, only she couldn't love him though she wished she could": Oh yes said Miss Butts, "I told him how dreadfully bad I was, but he only said, "dear child I know you better than you know yourself, & only wish I could

take you just as you are", & much more in the same
edifying strain. - - We came through from Charleston to Washington without stopping, where we
stayed over night, arriving in New York the following evening.

BREVOORT HOUSE
NEW YORK
APRIL 16TH. 1870
EASTER SUNDAY

IT HAS rained all day, & been a remarkably gloomy
Easter. General Hooker was here when we arrived,
looking much stronger & better than he did; he is
a splendid looking old gentleman & a great friend of
mine. Mr Skinner went to California last Teusday
to be gone two months. Uncle Nich is to be married
May 10; he looks very "swell" & happy, Miss
Wolfe's dress is point lace; We have not seen her
yet. I went to no 10 Gramercy Park on Saturday, &
had a charming visit. Susie Lawrance & Edith
Prescott, are both going to Europe. On Wednesday
I saw the "Hainites" ride at the Academy on the
Fifth Avenue; Helen Waggstaff rode a horse, on
which a sadle had never been laid before, & did it
splendidly too. Coming back I walked down with
the girls, & felt as if I was one of them again. Sister
has had one of her tonsels cut out & her throat is very
sore. Mr Churche's new picture of Jaimaca, is very

fine, but not equal to some of his others I think.—
I saw his "After glow", & did not like it much.
Sister & I spent a very pleasant hour at the "Academy of Design". There were quite a number of good
pictures, but most of them were such daubs. How
people who call themselves artists can daub on green
& blue together is beyond my comprehension.—

BREVOORT HOUSE
APRIL 20TH. 1870

MONDAY Sister & I took dinner at the Lows. On our
way to Brooklyn we stopped at the Shipping office
& secured our berths on board the "Ville de Paris"
which sails on the eleventh of June. (HORRORS.)
I like the Low's house immensely, it is so elegant, &
not a bit stiff. Gussie showed me his room, (the first
one belonging to a young man that I had ever seen.)
It was a perfect gem; crowded with knick-knacks &
pretty things, & the walls covered with pictures. And
then it was in such *perfect* order; I should have
thought it belonged to some lovely young lady.
Seth's room was larger, with more light, & less
fancy; he showed me his books, of which he is very
proud. After dinner Gussie & Hattie played duetts,
& Jay Pierrepont came in & had the sulks, because
he & John Jay Dubois had intended to spend the
evening with us (me) at the Brevoort house, & just

My Meeting with Susie Lawrence in a fifth Avenue church in New York.

as they were starting, Mr Pierrepont told him we
were dining at the Low's. The judicious Hooker
Hammersly was very anxious Sister & I should be
on his committee for the "Sheltering Arms" a great
bazaar just opened, & which is to last ten days.—
We went to see it, there was a fine collection of pictures, & tons, & tons of fancy work, which was horribly uninteresting. I saw a number of the "swell-
est" young men of New York, & (I say it sincerely
& without affectation,) I was bored inexpressably.
—Jay came over, I did not want to see him at all,
but I had to; he was deeply interested in my drawings, & altogether we had a very good time. The
Low's & Pierrepont's sail May 24 for Europe.—

### APRIL 30 1870

WE FINALLY left New York on Saturday, & glad I
was to get away. Mother & I stopped over three
hours, to see Jamie Clapp, who I had not seen since
he was three years old, in white frocks, & long curls.
We found him a fine manly little fellow of seven,
as large as any ordinary boy of eleven, not nearly as
handsome as formerly, though still very good looking, & really very bright, & original. We took a
walk together, & he made me buy him a stunning
blue cravat, & then announced that he wished
"Cousin Julia would buy him a watch-chain," &

really was so eloquent, that he half persuaded me
in to it.

We had a very nice visit in Utica; I spent two
nights with Nellie Devereux & I think she is very
sweet & pretty. I made Nich. Devereux's acquaintance, he is better looking & more sedate than Meredith; he took me riding every day, & it was great
fun, as I had never been driving with a young gentleman before. Aunt Devereux is as handsome as ever,
& a very fine old lady altogether. She always considered me a scape-grace, but came to the conclusion
I was QUITE presentable. She told us a good deal
about our Grand-Mother Clapp, Julia Hyde Butler
that was. It seems she had a most perfect figure,
marvelous hair, & glorious eyes.—Her other features were tolerable, but she was considered very
handsome. *Her* Mother was a Miss Avery, daughter
of Col. Avery & Miss Dolbeare of New London;
from whence come the "Dolbeare Arms" a Dukes
coronet, with five ostrich feathers, & a shield with
the motto in Latin, "Christ always," & which of
course rightly belongs in the family. The Dolbeares
were originally an old Welsh family, & now nearly
or quite extinct. Grand Mother Clapp was it seems
very independant, & no one could ever put her down,
or pass her by; & she was also a most exquisite
dancer. And her Mother, my great-grand-Mother,

*Butler,* was so fond of fine clothes, & dressed immensely for that time.—Utica is dull, quiet & old fashioned, though pleasant enough to visit. I have just been reading "Lucy Howard's Journal" by Mrs Sigourny, it presents such a contrast to mine. Her life was so quiet, day after day, year in & year out; I like the respect she shows for her parents, but her language appeares to me too studied, & her words are the longest she can find. She had evidently a great deal of book-knowledge, but seems lacking in what young girls almost always posess, namely, fun, humour, sarcasm, & enthusism. I dont think any young girl ever wrote such a journal.—

### HOME IN CHICAGO
#### MAY 9TH 1870

WE ARRIVED here Friday the 28 of April, & I stayed the first night at the Sherman House, & then came directly over here. I was amazed & delighted with the house, which has been almost entirely rebuilt since last summer at the gentle cost of $60,000. Every one says it is the handsomest house in Chicago, & every one in town, including many strangers, have been to see it. I am writing in what (to me) is the most perfect room I ever was in, My Studio. It fronts South & East, with the most beautiful view of the lake, & the most delicious window, so wide &

deep. It is irregular in shape also, & just the right size, with a genuine skylight, & private stair-case leading down into my dressing-room. There are two book-cases, & the loveliest closet; indeed it is just perfection. My real room down stairs is splendid, but I like the Studio best; down stairs I shall have to keep it in order, but here the door can be eternally locked if I choose, & no one can enter without permission. I dont believe there is another girl in the United States, or even in the world that has a real studio room built for *her;* it nearlly breaks my heart to think of leaving it all & going to Europe again, & I am so afraid I shall get to be like every-one else, & not want to come home, getting so accustomed to the life over there, that I shall care for nothing else. I like Chicago so much, so much better than any other place, & we have such a beautiful home, & it is all associated with Papa, & now to go & leave it all! If I only keep on liking it just as well, why then when I am an old maid I can always live here, & even *if* I *should* marry, My husband will have to live here, & there is one comfort in that, for then my children would live here too, & it would all go down in the family, it is too dreadful to think of strangers ever living here. The handsomest thing in the house is the hall, wainscoated, & finished beautifully in hard wood, & a clear sweep through the house, with a

vestibule at either end. The library & dining-room
are very large, & beautiful rooms, while the
"Butler's Pantry" is too charming. And as regards
bath-rooms, light, heat, there is nothing to desire.
The window glass is splendid & cost alone $3,000.
And still though the house has been so very much
improved, there is enough of the old building left,
to make us feel that it is always our old home. I
see Annie every day, & like her so much; And then
her great talent for music makes her doubly attractive in my eyes; she has played a great deal with
the Mendelsohne Quintette Club this winter, which
was a great honor of course.—Pumpkins's Mother
has just been here in Chicago, & I had quite a long
talk with her. He graduates June 17th, & now stands
no 18 in a class of 63; It seems he draws & paints
beautifully, & has been in that, ahead of all his
class; of course he rides splendidly & is perfectly
straight, besides being 5 feet $11\frac{1}{2}$ inches in hight.
He always danced very well, & played charmingly
on the piano, so altogether he must be quite accomplished. Madame had a very fine large photograph (one of Sarony's) in a beautiful frame of
the youth; & a young lady had previously told me,
that she had begged for the picture in vain. I
thought *I* should *not* ask in vain, & right before her,
& in a most indiffirent tone, I said that I thought she

might give it to me. I saw her hesitate, but then the
politic dame immediately consented, insisting that
I should keep the frame & all; which I accepted in
the coolest manner. He & his Mother are going
abroad for four months the first of July, so we shall
probably meet over there. We had a dashing call
from Gen. Phil. Sheridan the other night; he is
distingue, but frightfully ugly. (perhaps not frightfully but still anything but handsome.) He is very
short, (shorter than I.) *very* broad; & his eyes are
only long narrow holes. His head is most extraor-
diry shape. It is sunk between his shoulders & his
mouth is covered with a large moustache. He has a
nice foot, & good manners, an irish accent, & when
any-one makes a common-place remark or says
something that does not interest him, he says, "um,
um, yes, yes," in the most aggravating manner. He
has a good deal of the "General" about him, though
he is very modest, & well-bred; he is very complimentary to ladies, & evidently is a great admirer of
female beauty. He made me a great many sweet
speeches, none of which were very original.

IN MY STUDIO
MAY 26 1870

SINCE writing Sister has been to Utica & back, on one of her flying trips. Mr Kernan & Mr Mygalt are coming out to attend to the Executors & she went after them. I dont believe we shall leave America till the last of July! Monday week Annie Tinkham had a little surprise-party; I kept her, (unsuspicious victim) up in her room, while the others assembled in the parlor, & then when we went down & opened the door, there they were. The two Sturgeses, Min. Dunlap, Minnie Whitney, Lila Haughtling, Annie Larribee & brother, Jennie Tucker, Johnny Ellis, Jimmy Bowen, Myers boy, & Jewett boy, all snips, with one or two more.—I must have grown very old lately for the snips a little older than I, were such perfect boys, & I felt like their great Grand Mother at least; their ideas were bounded by *school* & base-ball on the one hand, & Racine College, & their own shyness on the other.—

They were awkward & clumsy any way.—& just snips!!!—Still we really had very good fun, & Annie was such a well bred hostess. But they were all so extremely young, I felt as if I had gone back several years. Annie was delighted with her surprise party, & we all voted it a great success. After they had all left, Annie & I went up stairs to bed, &

talked till we were worn out. I suppose that I shall
be well after a while, but at present it is tiresome to
the last degree. Everyone I meet has a diffirent cure,
that effected marvels with this one's cousin, or that
one's grandmother. And then the sighs & groans.
"And oh how strong & well you used to be," "& oh
how pale your are! & how big your eyes are," &
do you take port wine, brandy, iron, salt baths,
bordeaux, San Moritz, cod-liver-oil, raw meat, beef-
tea, sea-bathing, horse-back, donkey-back, brandy-
cock-tail, beer, ale, quinine, Nib, pyramids, &
egyptians.—Annie plays delightfully, her execution
is very good & she has a great deal of expression,
but still some how it does not *satisfy* me *completely*;
she interpretes correctly & her touch is light &
graceful, but still de temps en temps there is a note,
which is undeniably hard; & I have always had the
impression, great musician as she is, & much as she
cares & enjoys, & appreciates fine music, that she
does not love it, & that it does not give her as *intense*
pleasure as it does me.

Music is to me a sixth sense, above & beyond, &
apart from everything else; sometthing undefine-
able, inexpressible, which causes me the most intense feeling of mingled pain & pleasure; if it were
not almost or quiet irreverant, I should say that
the music in heaven will be the best part of it.

But these brilliant pieces, brilliantly executed I *cannot* enjoy. I always feel that if I could have heard the composers themselves, play these same brilliant pieces it might have been diffirent, & that in their understanding of their own works, there might have been a - - something, which would have made them delightful; but to hear one of Mrs Hoffman's pupils for instance, dash off a stunning piece all scales, octaves, trills, chords, lightning & thunder, with neither sentiment, or feeling, is simply disgusting.

### JUNE 2ND 1870

I HAVE just been skimming Disraeli's last novel "Lothaire" & it is simply horrid! If I were a great Statesman & had nothing better to do than to write such trash! I would give up. His plebian adoration of the English Aristocracy is disgusting.—We can not sail on June 17th because Mr Skinner is in California & wont come home till it is too late; so we shall July 23. My friend Pumpkins sails *June* 25 in the St Laurant, to be gone 3 months.

We are very quiet now a days & if I only felt well it would be very pleasant.—I get up late & paint in my *Studio* for two or three hours, have dinner read lounge around, play on the piano, & then about five drive up to the Park & down Wabash Ave: with plenty of fainting & hysterics in between.—I have felt miserably for the last few days, & they say if I'm not better I must go East, which would be a great shame, for all the girls except Fay Calhoun are coming in three weeks.—I see a good deal of Annie Tinkham, but not as much as I could wish, for she has so many lessons, & they keep her almost constantly occupied.

Uncle Nich, or "N. Devereux Clapp" as he now calls himself was married in N. York, to Miss Adèle Wolfe, on May 10th. Many of our relations were present, & the wedding though private, was very elegant, the presents particularly gorgeous!

She wore a dress coverd with lace, & also a real lace veil, & looked very pretty; every-one speaks well of her, & I hope sincerely she will be kind to Minnie & Jamie.

I think everything of Annie T. & she is just as nice & bright as she can be; I am at her hous frequently & feel almost as much at home there as here.

Our tastes are so similar, & both being devoted to Art, makes it charming. The family hope to spend the Summer in England, if Mr Tinkham's buisness will permit.—I thought I would cultivate Mrs Higginson's acquaintance a little, for as she is my God-Mother & it is high time I should know her.

So I took her driving & laid myself out to be agreeable. She appeared to enjoy it, & said she had

had a "feast of reason & flow of soul," when we got back; but nevertheless she is to Cynical, & sarcastic, to suit me, & then she has her highly interesting snip of a son, who is too stupid for anything.

Still poor woman she has had an *awfully* hard time, & that makes her satirical I suppose. When we first went out here with our poney-phaeton, there was not one to be seen with a "rumble", but now they are springing up like mushrooms, & are getting all the rage.

I have not read but one novel since we arrived, which I think is doing pretty well. I have been reading "Lamb", Tuckerman's book on American Artists, "Young's Night Thoughts, "Chemistry", "Pickwick", & the book of "Genisis", which are all very interesting. Some of Disraeli's "Curiositys of literature", with biographys of "Mrs Sigourney", "Ristori", "Theodosia Burr", "Mad. Necker", "Lady Anne Lindsey", "Maximilian" & others. I really am not well enough to read anything *deep*. A number of "lives of the Old Masters" I liked best of all. Scott's "Lord of the Iles" is charming.

ANNIE & I have spent the evening in my Studio, reading old letters, & talking of past present & future.

*She sails for Europe on the Sixteenth & leaves here next* Monday! It is my private opinion that we shall be abroad three years if not more. Annie comes back in November, after spending the Summer in England, but it will be many a long month before I see her again, & by that time we will be women, & girls no longer.

Now we are "where the brook & river meet."

She is my best friend now, & I do hope we shall not become estranged. So many girls with whom I have been intimate, I care for no more. Emily Healy is no more to me than any stranger, & I have piles & piles of her letters. Lila Moulton is the same thing! I can see now that I believed in them too much, & that neither are fine, brave, high-minded girls. Fannie Larned is another, & in all I have been just - - - - - disappointed!! I trust it will not be so with Annie! She is bright, clever, independant, & ambitious.

### JUNE 14TH

Mr Goldwin Smith went to church & dined with us on Sunday; we liked him emensely, & I never heard any one speak so delightfully. He has the English accent in perfection!

He gave us much interesting information about the aristocratic portion of English society, & told us about the Prince of Wales whose tutor he was at Oxford; & also about John Stuart Mill, Gladston, Lord Brome, & Lord Stanley, & others!

He said he admired any-one who was very rich, & yet studied; & he felt sure that if he had had £200,-000 lbs. a year like Lord Stanley he should have spent his time in reading novels. A remark I shall remember when I feel lazy!

*Charles Dickens died last Friday June 9th.*

### MONDAY, JUNE 20TH 1870
### CHICAGO

Annie T. is on the deep blue sea, the ever rolling sea, she was wild about going. I know she will have a delightful time & enjoy it so much, it will do her a great deal of good besides.

The only young gentlemen in this big town, who merit the slightest consideration at the present moment, are the two Mr Whitehouse, (Frank & William). I meet them driving often, & William who has

a very "swell drag" has repeatedly asked me to go
driving with him, & poor me, though I want to go
ever so much, I always refuse, because I dont think
it is quite proper to go driving with young gentlemen.

11 O'CLOCK AT NIGHT IN
BED!

AND yet all most all the girls here & elsewhere do
it! I am always glad afterwards that I stood firm,
though at the time it is very hard! Saturday I took
the interesting Minnie Whitney in the phaeton to the
Park.—It is looking lovely now, & is beginning to
be very fashionable. Mr W. Whitehouse was there,
he got out of his drag, & we had a long talk. This
afternoon he brought me "blackwoods Magazine",
with a long & capital criticism on "Lothair". Ma.
& Sis. were out and as he only asked for me, I received him, & he made a very nice call. We went
over to the bishop's church Sunday Eve. & W. W.
played the organ very well. It seems so queer that
a young man 35 years old, should be attentive to me,
heretofore, all my "particular friends" except Jack
Foster & Gussie Low have been snips. PS, (Mr
Bigelow was 24.)

I received some time since a very clever note, &
a perfect jewel of an alligator made of pure gold,
from Gussie Low. "To console me for the loss of

the other one". I was perfectly amazed, & really very much pleased; he is so queer, one never knows what he will do next.—

Mrs Sheldon died yesterday.—

Pumpkins graduated No 28. on the 17' of this month;

I was miserable last week; & I think I have rather lost than gained since I got home. I supposed that once on my native heath, I should be all right.

### JUNE 22ND 1870

TOMORROW I am going to leave my beloved Chicago for another long while, years perhaps! I am not well here, & I think it is my bounden duty to go away, & not get any sicker!

So I am going down to Utica by myself, with Ernestine of course for propriety, to stay till Ma. & Sis. can finish their buisiness, & join me.

The executors have behaved anything but well of late, (it is too long to write about here) & Mr Kernan, who is now our Lawyer is coming out, to see into the matter! It seems hard to bid my Studio good-bye, & leave this lovely house, besides everything else! When we shall come back, is more than I know; I hope & trust I shall not be entirely weaned from my own home, & prefer Europe to anything else, on the Earth or under it.

UTICA, N. Y.
SUNDAY JUNE 26' 1870

HERE I am in this delightfully stupid place, horribly bored half the time, & rather amused the rest. Aunt Devereux is very kind, but fearfully formal & particular, & Cousin Cornelia is a very old maid, one would never dream she had been married!— Frank Kernan, Nicholas Devereux & Meridith were in to night, & *they* were nervous at my sitting out on the steps with my own cousins.

Meridith gave me a long drive last evening, & I am going with Frank tomorrow. Still, I feel as if I were at boarding-school, & Aunt D.—the teacher; I hate to be tied up so. I am as solem as an owl all the time; but I really feel stronger than I did at home. All my girl cousins are coming from school on Teusday, for which I am devoutly thankful. Aunt Butler is here, sick & feeble, but convelacent; rather a good looking old maid.

TEUSDAY JUNE 28' 1870.

JUST for fun I am going to write down the names of the boys, snips & young gentlemen, who are, or have been my particular friends. Nearly all I should be happy to see again, there are a few who for one reason or another I do not like perticularly now, but these are exceptions, & I shall mark them with a x. The others I know well, & are all very particular friends. Of course these are all *my* friends, entirely apart from Sisters, & all of whom except Robbie Dickey (though still he ought to be counted) have shown themselves at diffirent times, particularly interested in my humble self.

June 1870

My Particular Male friends
as they stand up to the present time.

| | |
|---|---|
| Abott Kinney. | Willie Mygalt. |
| Johnny Dodge. x | Charles Conningham. |
| Walter Larned x | Mr Divitt. |
| Aurthur Ryerson. | Charles Bigelow. |
| Dudley Higginson. | Randall Curell. |
| Willie Larned. | Mr Bosworth. x |

Jay Pierrepont.

Colonel Bonaparte.   July 1870

| | |
|---|---|
| Gussie Low | W. F. Whitehouse. |
| Seth Low. | Meridith Devereux. |
| Nich. Devereux. | Jack. Foster. |
| Frank Kernan. | Robbie Dickey. |

*Old or Married Gentlemen*

| | |
|---|---|
| George Smith | Capt. Tucker. |
| Gen. Hooker | Gen. Bloomfield |
| Gen. McIvor | Mr Fairbank. |
| Dr Bronson | Count Vanderlyn. |

Grand-pa Sturges.

UTICA
JULY 5TH. 1870

YESTERDAY the fourth, was slow, as the fourth of
July always is. I spent the day at the Devereux's, &
had a very good time altogether.—I played, painted,
& sent Nich to buy me some fireworks. In the evening we fired them off, which was very amusing.
Mollie set fire to her dress with a roman candle, &
narrowly escaped, by Nich Kernan's throwing his
coat around her. I have just read Mrs Gasgells life
of Charlotte Brontë, & enjoyed it immensely, almost
as much as Jane Ayer.—Meredith has gone into the
country for a few days.—I cant decide whether I
like him or not; though he is very attentive, & we
have very good times together. Mollie D, is very
pretty though her nose is rétroussé. She has lovely
eyes, & her mouth & teeth are charming, & added to
this such a pretty color. She will be snapped up in
no time, by some horrid man or other, not half good
enough for her.—I think Nellie will be still prettier,
though she is not now. The Devereuxs are a wonderfully good looking family, & just as lovely & charming as possible, but there is no superfluity of a
slightly agreeable quality, & that is - - *brains*. -
Cousin Ellen is a wonderful woman, in the way she
has brought up her family. I wish Aunt D. had a
long black satin gown, trimmed with lace about the
neck, she would look so handsom in it. She thinks

men, are as unselfish as women; I dont! It must be
awfully slow living here all the year round, I'm
thankful it is not my lot. It is no wonder that
cousin Cornelia is billious, & as yellow as gold; I
never saw anyone eat as she does; for tea she will eat
cucombers, tomatoes, bread, meat, eggs, preserves,
biscuit, & cake, all one on top of another.

JULY 10—1870

MAMMA & Ernestine arrived today, & in about two
weeks we expect to start again on our travels. We
are nothing but a family of "wandering jews".—
Mamma looked as fresh as a rose, when she arrived,
I am so glad that she looks so young & handsome,
every-one admires her, I must say that I dont think
we three, Mamma, Sister, & I, are a very bad looking family. And then we are all so diffirent, Sister
& I especially being diametrically opposite. I am
thankful she is fair & I am dark, I hate Sisters, who
are repititious of each other! Mamma is about
five feet four, not too fat, but just right. She hasn't
a grey hair though she is fifty-two years old, & her
complexion is smooth as satin, with a lovely color,
like a young girl.—Her eyes are brown, & very
large, & set in her head in a peculiar manner. Her
nose & mouth are good though not regular.—Altogether she is very handsome, & every one says as a
young girl, she was a beauty.

### JULY 17TH 1870

FRANCE has declared war against Prussia, & the troops are on the march! My visit in Utica is drawing to a close, & altogether I have enjoyed it very much. My young gentlemen cousins are so attentive that it is really embarrasing. And there is always a question, as to whether Nich. or Meredith shall escort me home. I have four invitations to drive on hand now, & each is mad if I go with the other. I have spent this, my last Sunday at the Devereux, & enjoyed it very much. They have a lovely croquet ground, & Nich. plays very well.—Tomorrow I shall stay all night. Sister is at Richfield with Mollie Devereux for company.—I think Aunt D. is coming round, she treats me with great consideration, & really appears quite fond of me. I knew she would, ha! ha!—Nich. Kernan is the queerest creature, but his beautiful teeth make up for a great deal.— I have upset them pretty generally I think

### NEW YORK

IT IS awfully hot; we left Utica during a violent shower of rain, the snips were wet through, coming down to see us off;—Mamma & Sis. left Aunt Devereuxs enveloped in red table-covers, instead of waterproofs.—

BETWEEN BREST & HAVRE
ON BOARD THE
STEAMER LAFAYETTE
AUG. 4. 1870

WE HAVE had a long passage, & this is the thirteenth day; but still it has been not only pleasant but jolly. —It was awfully hot in New York & we were glad to get away. Mr Mygalt was afraid to let Willie come on account of the war, & Sam Johnson went in the Scotia.—The Utica people were nervous of course, & Mamma also, was morally convinced that we would be captured by a Prussian man-of-war; & they all thought us rather crazy to start, when war had just been declared in Europe.—We found something less than a hundred first class passengers, a very small number, & only one American family, the Parkers of Newark, & one or two married men, the only young gent (avalible) was Colonel, Jerome Napoleon Bonaparte.—

Things did not look very promising at first, but wonder of wonders, none of us were sea-sick. Sister took a great fancy to Mlle Paradol, who is very sweet, & quite pretty.—Poor girl, she is having a dreadful time.—We had great fun at the Captain's table, there were three french officers, Col. Bonaparte, the Captain, & two other men.—They were immensely excited about the war! Col Bonaparte was not introduced to us till Friday, & since then, he hardly left Sister & I night or day.

Miss Parker was also introduced, & behaved in a perfectly idiotic manner. Five minutes after he first spoke to her, she asked permission to taste his tea; that was the beginning, & he was so disgusted, that though perfectly polite, he ignored her completely from that time, & yet much as he snubbed her, she would join us, & sit for three or four hours; and on the least provocation, join in the conversation, & say *such* things! I never, never, never, saw *anybody* behave so.—

We liked the Colonel very much, & that is a great deal for me to say.—

He has the most magnificent figure I ever saw!!!

Six feet one, to begin with, & his chest in proportion; & feet & hands that would be remarkable small, & well formed on an *ordinary* sized man.

Then he has a charming voice, & such elegant manners. He is the funniest man, & I havn't laughed so much in a year. I wouldn't tell him my first name, so he dubbed me Mlle Alphonsine, & seemed to enjoy it hugely.—

He can talk in the most pious & persuasive manner, till you would think him a perfect saint, & then to hear him go on, about his Mother the church, & his father the Pope!

He is colonel of "les dragons de l'imperatrice",
& when on duty wears a gilt helmet with a black
horse's tail streaming in the wind, green & gold
uniform, & red trousers.—He told us various interesting anecdotes, on widely diffirent subjects.
How the Empress looks, & how to make brandy-
cock-tail; How marriages are arranged in France,
& how he entered Harvard as a Junior before going
to West Point, & was brought up before "the faculty" for having a private cock-pit in his rooms.—
How he set the McCoom's girls a-going, in Paris,
& the many virtues of his private valet de chambre,
who procured a piano at two o'clock at night on five
minutes notice, etc, etc, etc. But the most interesting
thing that he told us about, was the Battle of
Balaclava, at which he asisted & the charge of the
light brigade which he saw.—I will put it in his own
words.—"Just before the charge was made, I was
sent by the commander of the French forces, to compliment the English General Lord          , on the
charge his *heavy brigade* had just made."

"He of course was very much flattered, & while we
were talking young Noland came up, & presented
Lord          with a paper. He read it, & then turned
to Noland & said, "but where the devil does he mean
me to charge."—

"Noland looked up, & said in the most insolent

manner, "I dont know m'i lord, but if you follow me, *I*'ll show you the enemy."

"I thought Lord            would blow his brains out on the spot; but instead he turned as white as death, & gave the order to-*charge*. And oh it was a magnificent sight to see those eight hundred Englishmen splendidly mounted, charge without hesitation, into the face of death, into the mouth of hell! There was n't the faintest shadow of a chance; not the faintest!! Noland was almost the first one shot, I saw him on a litter a few minutes after; the whole thing did not occupy more than fifteen or twenty minutes. And they came stragling back in little batches of four or five, & the horses perfectly frantic galloping all over the plain."

"I saw Lord          a little while after & oh! how *mad* he was, convulsed with rage, & in the most dreadful state. He had the order Noland had given in his hand, & he showed it to me! "Do you see - - - e - - - - - - *THAT sir*, tha-t - - - p-a-per, sir, I would n't give that *pa-per* for *five hundred* thous - - and pounds - - -."

PARIS. AUGUST. 7TH

THERE is the jolliest row here; the people go down the rue de la paix shouting the Marseillaise, thousands at a time, with cries of vive la nation, & Olivier. They are horibly excited, because yesterday there was a false report of a victory. - - The flags were hung out, & the greatest joy & enthusiasm prevailed, when it was announced that it was all a mistake, fabricated by some speculators at the Bourse.

The people were beside themselves with disappointment; they tore down the inside of the Bourse, & would have Lynched the originaters of the report if they could have got hold of them.—

In fact two corps of the army under Gen. Mac-Mahon were surrounded yesterday by the Prussian army, & forced to retreat.—

Colonel Bonaparte much to my astonishment, called this morning & most gorgeously put up. The red shirt, brown coat, & yellow gloves of the Lafayette had all disappeared, & he was perfectly dressed, in the garments of woe.

A deep crape band encircled his beaver, immaculate black gloves, & neck-tie, & the rest of his costume was blacker still.—He looked *extremely* well, & was ever so nice. He had just seen the Empress, or "his sovereign" as he calls her, & she will not permit him to go to the war, & he is very much annoyed.— as I should think he might be. - - - Minnie has spent her vacation with her new Mamma, & I guess she likes her very much.

AUGUST 12. 1870

THE French have suffered three successive defeats; & the people are discouraged & bewildered. Gold here has gone up to five per. cent. The city is under Marshal Law, & squads of soldiers, with fixed bayonettes clear the streets nightly. It is very amusing to see the people scatter at the first roll of the drums! The Empress regent is almost alone at the Tuilleries.

AUGUST 18TH

THE French have been defeated three successive times, & have retreated to Chalons, almost halfway to Paris. But they have fought gloriously; at the battle of Woerth there were 37,000 French, againts 140,000 Prussians, & they held there ground, five to one, from seven in the morning, until six at night. If that wasn't magnificent! The fortifications around Paris are nearly completed, if the Prussians come they will destroy the Bois immediately. The people have no back-bone; instead of leaving all private dissensions till the danger is past, & uniting heart & soul to save their country, they spend their time quarrelling as to who shall govern. They expelled Olivier, & Palikao became minister of war. And they had the most disgraceful rows in the Chambers; Jules Favre, red hot republican, said the Emperor should abdicate; & then some one else re-

marked that Favre should be shot. Col Bonaparte is
infinitely disgusted with them. he has been here four
times in ten days, & he "never makes visits". What
does he come for? !!! I should like to know! It is im
possible to get gold, & trade is at a stand-still. Sister
has a nasty attack of rheumatism, & we can not go to
Switzerland till she is better.—The _Colonel_ usually
comes about half past eight, & stays until eleven. We
have very jolly calls, Mamma, he, & I. I dont see
why he comes, there is nothing very interesting when
he gets here. I dont believe he is much used to young
ladies, for he treats me with the most profound respect, though he is an awful teaze. Admiral Farra-
gut is dead, & general Thomas, three months since.

GENEVA
SEPT. 4TH 1870

SISTER forbid my telling the Colonel when we were
going. He spent Teusday evening with us, & was
ever so nice; we gave him some tea & were very
jolly; he asked when we were going, & Sister said,
in a day or two. "Oh yes I shall see you when I come
again" he said; & so she would n't let me say good
bye, & on Thursday we left. Because he liked me, &
came to see me nine times in three weeks, Sister
must needs pretend she didn't like him., but it was
all pretense, for she saw him every time she was well

enough. The truth was, she feared I might take a
fancy to the Colonel; but I never thought it was *me*
he liked, till she & Mamma put it into my head.—I
know that I shall never see another man with *such a
figure* if I live a hundred years. - - - *Now? !!!*

GRAND HOTEL VEVEY
SEPT 23RD 1870

MINNIE is as tall as I, & as broad, & simply enormous for her age, as she is just fourteen.—I think
she has improved in these fifteen months, but she has
not changed any.—She is very young for her years,
& has seen & experianced so little, that at present I
am far more than two years ahead of her. When she
is twenty-eight, & I thirty, there will be far less diffirence. Napoleon, after the battle of Sedan, yielded
him—prison to the king of Prussia, and 80,000
Frenchmen laid down their arms.—Strasbourg &
Toul have surrendered, & Paris is now one immense
fortress.—If Paris surrenders, I shall be utterly
crestfallen! There is no reason why it can not main-
tain itself, fortified, & well provisioned as it is; & if
the Parisians havn't sufficient patriotism to remain
united while the enemy is at their gates, they deserve
the contimpt of every-one. I wish *I* had command of
Paris; any man that presumed to utter a word that
might cause discord, would be instantly shot! & all

the women, children, & useless cowardly men I
would send into the interior; that they might not fill
up the city, & consume the provisions—. Bazaine
must be having a pleasant time, shut up in Metz
with a hundred-thousand men! The Prussians *mod-
estly* ask for Alsace, Lorraine, & one of the forts
overlooking Paris; what could be more humiliating.
—The style in which girls at the present time try to
captivate young-men, is certainly peculiar! It appears to me, that a nice young girl, well born, & well
bred, should under all circumstances be lady-like &
reserved.—She may be lively, & yet dignified,
pretty & not affected, & clever without appearing
conscious of it.—If a girl knows that she possesses
any particular thing, which makes her attractive, it
is far better to let other people find it out, than to
continually remind them of it.—All girls like to be
admired, & to receive attention; but if they can not
obtain it, without running after the men, they had
much better do without. There are very few young
men, who can resist the temptation to amuse themselves, by making a giddy girl do & say foolish
things; they will dance attendance on her, & pretend to approove, that which they secretly despise,
but at the same time they are very particular as regards the manner in which their Sister's behave.—If
a girl is treated with too much familiar it is *almost*

always her own fault; men will go just as far as she will let them!—And indeed I dont blame them for I should do just the same if I were a man; I am sure I was intended to be one, & if I had been, would n't I have been a flirt? I should have been devoted to every pretty girl that came along,—& I would never have spoken to ugly woman if I could have helped it.—But then some girls are such geese, & they always defeat their own object, when they attempt that kind of thing.—If a man wants to see you he will come & see you, & if he wants a private conversation, he will manage to have a private conversation; they know very well what they are about, & do not wish any assistance.—But girls seem to think that it is their part to make opportunities.—

PEOPLE AT THE
GRAND HOTEL VEVEY
SEPTEMBER 1870.

| | |
|---|---|
| Ogdens. | I like very well |
| Mr & Mrs Lee | "　" pretty well |
| Mr & Mrs Hunneywell. | |
| | I like pretty well |
| Mrs Livingstone | - - - - - - - - - - |
| Murry Livingston | |
| | detestable, odious! |
| Francias | no.— |

| | |
|---|---|
| McCarthy's | Yes. |
| Warrens | no. |
| Crosbies | so, so. |
| Mr. Burgen | well enough. |
| H. Hammersly. | yes  "  " |
| Miss Beech. | no. |
| Mr Myer | yes.— |
| Mr Sheppard | no. |
| Morris | yes |
| Miss Post. | no |
| Little (Mr) | - - - - |
| *Pells.*— | *no* |
| Mrs Phoenix | - - - - |
| Mrs Bishop | - - - - |
| Mrs White | - - - - |
| M D'Hauteville | so. so. |
| Boyeds.— | *no* |

This is a charming hotel; we have croquet, music, dancing, walking parties, excursions, whist, sketching etc. etc. There are a number of young people also, & it is really quite jolly.

The day before Yesterday, we went up to Bex, a party fifteen, they gave us a stunning dinner. There is a man here, Francia by name, that bothers me a great deal. He has been rather attentive ever since we first arrived, but only within the last few days has

he become too much so. At Bex he sat next me at
dinner, & talked no end of trash. He plays & paints
very well, & has been doing my picture all the time
lately; *from memory*, in oils, & twice in water-colors.—He says the most extraordinary things; "that
he will never paint another picture in which he will
not put me", etc, etc, etc. Well, coming home from
Bex, he was so demonstrative, that I was very much
annoyed; we managed to get into a diffirent "com-
partiment", & on arriving I came up stairs immediately, & did not go down all day yesterday.—Last
evening I dined up stairs, & after dinner Mamie
Ogden or "my "fiancée" as I call her, came up to
beg me to go down & see the dancing. I did not want
to, & while we were talking in the hall, up comes a
servant, & presents me with a tremendous white rose,
done up like a bouquet, & "Mr Francia's compliments", I was so angry that the rose was immediately torn in pieces, & the débris thrown out of the
window.

Down stairs I was cooly polite, but made no mention of the rose. "Would I dance"? "No I didn't
care to this evening." "Did I feel well"? "Not particularly" etc. Finally he withdraws, dances once
or twice, & then smokes furiously in a corner for the
rest of the evening! - - And just as mad!

## MONDAY OCT 3, 1870

I HAVE kept up stairs for the last two days. Mr Francia laid in wait when I went into dinner but he gained nothing by it. The rest of the evening I played whist in Miss Beeche's room, with Messers Myer & Sheppard. We beat the rubber! Ella Low Pierrepont has a little girl, ten days old.—

## FRIDAY OCT. 7TH 1870

I LEFT the table d'hote before desert, so that I might come up to my own room before that odious Francia had finished his dinner. They are going on Sunday & I am so thankful, I shall be ill if they stay any longer. I havn't been in the garden, or down stairs in the daytime for more than a week, for fear of meeting that odious creature. I have done everything in my power to make him leave me alone; I have avoided & shunned him, & been fridged and cross, & he is as horrid as ever. I detest him!

He sent me some of his charming works of art to-day, with a picture he had done of me from memory; perfectly odious.—

He cant draw atall, & yet so conceited!

Yesterday Mamma & I drove to Castle Blauney; it is perfectly preserved, & many hundred years old. I sketched it in pencil there, & did it in color at home. Paris is entirely surrounded, by the enemy, &

intelligence can only be transmitted by balloon. The king of Prussia now makes his head-quarters at Versailles.

Strasbourg has surrendered, with a garrison of 17,000 men. Napoleon is at Williamshoe, & the Empress & Prince Imperial are in some old manor house in England.—

NICE OCTOBER 22, 1870
HOTEL DES ANGLAIS

ONE by one the people left Vevey, until we were reduced to Mr Mc'Carty, who kindly sent me some bonbons & roses. I cant say I was deeply grieved to part with any of the people! & after all there are so few that one cares to meet again.—We amused ourselves, with dodging Stouty, who was staying at hotel Byron & who haunted Vevey like "Banquo's ghost." The Ex-Queen Isabella. (As for Francia the detestable, I did not speak to him for two days before he left, nor did I bid him good bye.) Queen Isabella was staying at the Métropole. I was standing apart, in the hall when she came down stairs, for her ride. She looked at me attentively, & then made a very gracious bow, which I returned with equal dignity.—She is immensely stout, & has large features. It was a rainy afternoon, & the costume, was to say the least mal-apropos.—A lilac-silk walking dress, ornamented with white lace, surmounted by a

black velvet cloak, with gold fringe; besides there
was a sky-blue bonnet.

### OCTOBER 31ST 1870

METZ has capitulated, & they say Bazaine has *surrendered*, with a hundred & 80 thousand men! Poor
France! what suffering & what desolation. Defeated!
betrayed, & crushed. When one think's how her glory
has been exalted, & her army esteemed invincible.
And now! Paris the sun of all France, clouded with
civil dissensions, & hidden behind the bulworks of
the enemy.—

### NOVEMBER 20TH

RUSSIA threatens to throw up the treaty of 1856, &
another great contest is possible. The Winter has
come on early everywhere; it must be delightful for
the Prussians outside of Paris, to be beseigeing it,
in the mist & fog. Rather rheumatic I should say;
they will have enough of it before they get through.
Bismarck & Thiers, tried to arrange an armstice, but
it fell through. The French had one decided success,
when they retook Orleans the other day.

Nice, is most most indiscribably dull just now, &
very empty for this time of year. About ten days
ago, I went out one morning to take a little walk!
The sun was pretty hot, but I had on a "Nice hat"
and a double parasol in my hand. I walked on very
complacently, thankful to be feeling a little stronger

& brighter than I had in some time; when on the other side of the "jardin Anglais" I began to feel queer in my head. But ever since I was first taken ill fourteen months ago, I have had a continuation, of faint turns, & chills; & so, as feeling queer was no novelty, Sister & I sat down to rest. Presently the dull pain in my head became more sensibly felt, & a chill began to creep over me. It was high time to go home & home I went. Friday morning at noon, & until the next Friday I suffered more acute pain than I ever did before! Doctor Travis, the English physician who was sent for, told me immediately that I had had a sun-stroke! & of course it told much more heavily on me, that it would have done on a well person. I began with a most fearful sick head-ach which lasted forty-eight hours; the pain then went into the cords of my neck, & from thence to my back. It upset my stomache completely, & altogether has I fear much retarded my ultimate recovery. I think I am in much the same state as when I returned from Florida last spring. I was better then, but I ran down very much at home during the summer.

FRIDAY, 25TH NOVEMBER, 1870

WE HAVE been here more than a month, and I have managed so neatly, that yesterday was the first time I had to speak to Pequee. He has gone to & fro be-

fore the house every day since he first knew we had
arrived. He has only missed once, even in all this
bad weather. I have only driven up & down the
"promenade, where all he could do was to bow
sulkily, & when he called, the ladies were particularly engaged.

Sissy & Mrs Francia keep coming to see us, & are
so *very* affectionate. Finally yesterday afternoon,
we took chairs on the Promenade, & looked at the
people. We were not seated two minutes before
Pequee came along, with his pot hat on, a rose in his
button-hole, yellow gloves, & his dog.—He was as
pale as a ghost, & looked like a fright! ough!—Of
course he shook hands all around; I had given Sister
private enjunctions not to ask him to sit down, so he
stood up, & there was a little dismal conversation
about nothing atall. He stayed as long as he decently
could & then rushed off with his usual frantic walk.

The Promenade is quite gay now, on sunny afternoons

### DECEMBER. 4. 1870

Mrs Little & her son have been here, & the Franklin
also; they have now gone on to Naples, but they will
come back before long.—Commodore Rogers came
to see us, he seemed very nice.—Piquée affords me
infinite amusement. In the parlor I have a chair so
arranged that I can sit at the window, & see every

one that passes on the Promenade, which is very
amusing. And every afternoon between three & four,
Mr Piquée Francia makes his appearance. He always looks up to see if I am in the window, & I
always look the other way.—A man must be half an
idiot to act as he does.—Indeed he is so effeminate,
& such a flatterer, that I just despise him, with his
red shirts, & green neck-ties, for he does dress like
a perfect fiend.—The lazy lives these foreigners
lead, are enough to disgust any one.—

Mr Little is a most peculiar person,—he told me
he had never asked for any one's photograph in his
life, unless out of politeness when they had asked
for his.—I have painting lessons with Mr Vigna,
his water-colors are splendid, so bold & free, very
diffirent from the over-worked & finished English
style.—I am only able to have about two lessons a
week, & Mamma & Sister will not let me work between times. I have got a piano which is a great
consolation, though I am not strong enough to play
much; There seems to be a fatality which prevents
my ever becoming a musician of any consequence,
though I am so fond of it. Except the six months
with Mlle Steiner, I have never been able to continue with a good teacher, we are always travelling,
& always have been, & just as sure as I can practice
for four months, there will be six months when I can

do nothing. I was in a good way when I left Mlle Pelets, & now for two years I have not been able to do a single thing, & I really think it is pretty hard!

### NICE
#### DECEMBER 28TH 1870

MAMMA presented me this morning with an emerald ring. And Sister gave me an hundred dollars in gold. I slept till eleven this morning, & when I awoke I could not believe I was really seventeen years old. Seventeen rather eventful years take them altogether. I have been twice to Florida, & three times to Europe. I have been to two boarding-schools, & gained a great many friends in diffirent ways. Have been run-away with twice, & had my portrait painted. I have learned how to faint, & have inheireted a fortune. Have been through a long illness & had a terrible sorrow! And I might have been married if I had choosen.

On the other hand I have never had on a long dress, or been into society as a young-lady; Nor in the conventual form, have I been to my first ball.— I have never given my photograph to a young man, or any other souvenir either, nor have I made my hair uneven by distributing locks, among my friends. I have never waved my handkerchief, to a male biped on the other side of the street, or appointed a rendevous on my way to school.—I have never sworn eternal friendship to any one, nor written poetry since I was eleven years old.

I have never fancied myself in love, even in extreme youth, with either a little boy in knickerbockers, or a *man* with side-whiskers.—

Nor can I say I have been much in want of attention from the opposite sex. I can not remember when I *first* ran away from them, & their gallantries. I have a great many nice *friends,* & what I am chiefly proud of, *"old gentlemen" friends,* whom I can look up to with respect.

Besides there are number who are particularly fond of me, & whom I particularly hate.

#### (CONTINUED NEXT DAY)

LAST night I took tea at the Francias! I went because it was the only way in which I could have "un peu de distraction" on my birthday. I wore my Paris black silk, & coral ornaments, with my hair rolled over a cushion in front, & chatelaine braids behind; I looked tolerably respectable, & felt rather curious as to the result of my visit.

In the salon I found, Mon, Madame & Sissy. My welcome was the reverse of fridged; & the fuss about keeping me warm & near the fire, became rather a bore. Presently in walks the illustrious son & heir,

dressed decently enough, but for a detestable pair
of pantaloons. He was in a most aimiable mood, but
it was rather fatigueing, talking to four people at
once. I wanted Sissy to sing but Sissy was capricious
& would'nt sing, so Piquée played some of his compositions, & presented me with several, which really
were not so bad. Then we had tea, & looked at pho-
tographs, & I was a little bored, they were so op-
presively amiable. At ten I rose to go. Piquée
opened the carriage door, & then as usual intended
to shake hands. I ignored that part of the pro-
gramme entirely, & jumped into the carriage without looking at him. When I looked up to say good
night; he had fled discomfited, & there was only Joe,
who had evidently, hugely enjoyed his brother's defeat smiling maliciously in the lamp light.—

MIDNIGHT
LAST NIGHT OF THE YEAR 1870

How many thousands of families, that were happily
united last New Year's Eve must be suffering to
night.—How many homes this war has ruined. How
strangely things are situated at the present moment!
Paris beseiged by 300,000, Prussians reduced so,
that it is said even all the rats & cats have been con-
sumed, & they have eaten the animals of the zoolog-
ical garden. The Pope is shut up in the Vatican, &

refused on Christmas to perform service in St. Peters. King William has become Emperor of Germany. Rome belongs to Victor Emanuel! The Duke of Aosta has just been elected king of spain. The Empress is at Chislehurst, & the Ex Emperor at Williamshoe. 350,000, french-men are prisoners in Germany.—France is a republic! This year has gone extremely fast; & yet I am still sick, though much better than twelve months ago. I have spent the last two hours in drawing a ball, out of my head. with Mamma on one side & Sister on the other. Mamma is fifty two, Sister twenty-five, & I am seventeen. This evening being New Years Eve, I was most disagreeably surprised. Mr Francia had the impudence to send me a bonbonnière, even after the way in which he has been snubbed. It is too much! oh how furious I was when it came.


### JAN. 20' 1871

LAST Saturday there was a small matinée on the Franklin, which we enjoyed very much.


### FEBRUARY 8'. 1871

LAST week Mrs Boyd gave a ball for the officers, & it was decided that I should go, & wear a *long* dress! Of course I felt extatic when I was finally dressed, with a yard & three-quarters of ruffeled muslin,

trailing behind.—I had never worn a train before,
& at first I was afraid I might step on it. But I found
that I did not mind it in the least.—We went with
the Francias, & everybody was there. It was a very
pretty ball & I had a most stunning time; a number
of new officers were introduced to me, & I was engaged for every dance, & asked for a great many
more.—Hattie Warren was there also, in her first
long dress.—So many officers come to see us now
that it is a great bore; there were six in last night
when we did not expect any one. General Sheridan
arrived here last night; he drove with Sister & I all
the afternoon; we drove to the "Place d'Armes" to
see a base-ball match between the Franklin & Plymouth. Everyone stared at the General as though he
had been a pearl of great price. He has had a most
splendid time, & was with the Prussian army, for
more than two months, & he has been received everywhere with the greatest distinction.—Last Thursday,
Feb. 9th we had a most stunning matinée on the
Franklin. The General was first received on board,
& then the dancing begun. I was promenading with
Mr Dunnell (a very nice fellow) when much to my
amazement, the General who so far had done nothing, comes up & asks me to dance Of course I said
yes, & after the round dance, he asked me for the
next which was a quadrille  He is very punctilious &

dances avec un grand air, & of course I did the same. I did not dance any more round dances except with him, but I had just as good a time for they all asked me just the same, & we promenaded instead. I enjoyed myself most, sitting on a piano-stool on the gun-deck, with my three particular friends, Dunnell, Burroughs & Berry.——Gen Sheridan asked me again for the last waltz, & then he asked me if I would wear his colors? Whereupon he took off the badge of the army of the Shenandoah which he had on, & transfered it to me. We all went on the same boat together, & as the General stepped in, there was a prolonged cheer from the sailors, who had climbed into every conceiveable place on the rigging. He bowed in return, & seemed very much gratified.

SUNDAY FEB. 19TH 1871

LAST Monday we went down to a matinée on the "Guèrriere"; the ship enclosed with flags, & dressed with flowers, looked beautiful; the officers from the Plymouth & Juniata were there, dancing with all their might, their time was short as their respective ships were to sail at four o'clock. Mr Dillingham & his little English friend Miss Michael, were getting near the end of their flirtation, & danced & promenaded violently.——My friend Mr Dunnell was going also. & he pretended to feel very bad too; he is

only twenty, but one of those gay & festive youths
that develop early.—a nice jolly fellow though—&
we had great fun.—

| | |
|---|---|
| Littles | Gen. Sheridan |
| Warrens | Gen. Forsyth |
| Francias | Mr. Dunnell |
| Boyds | Capt. Breeze |
| Williamsons | Capt. Luce |
| Mrs Bird | Capt. Parker |
| Miss Shaw | Admi. Boggs |
| Pells | Mr. Folger |
| Twells | Rogers |
| Campbells | Berry |
| Trelawneys | Wilson |
| McCalls | Burroughs |
| Boreels | Phelps |
| Langdons | Seymour |
| Hendersons | Corrie |
| Fellows | Hinkes |
| Kanes | Little |
| Schemmerhorn | Mason |

Sister and Capt Breeze meanwhile were having
a *very* interesting time on the "poop," & sundry
other couples were doing the same. Finally the time
came, & we said good bye, for the last time, a thing
I hate; the Plymouth was only a few hundred yards

distant, & she was already moving when her officers stepped on board. She steamed slowly out to sea, while our band played "old lang syne" & "the girl I left behind me. I never saw anything more romantic & picturesque in my life; the warm golden atmosphere, the deep blue water, "Ville Franche" & the mountains in the background; the girls in their bright dresses, the gay flags, the music, all combined; seemed more like a scene in a romance, than an incident in real life.—From the "poop" of the "Guerriere" where we were all standing, we waved our handkerchiefs to our friends on the Plymouth, as they went further & further away, & by the time we started to return home, we could see nought but a faint white speck on the horizon.—Piquée goes to all the matinées, but he never dances any more, & spends most of his time staring at me. I never speak to him if I can help it.—On Thursday we had the last grand matinée on the Franklin. I had a splendid time, in fact I think each one was nicer than the other. I have seen more of Mr Berry lately than of any else; such a nice fellow, I dont know when I have seen any one I like as well. I noticed him the very first matinée, he was on duty that day, & taking observations on deck, where I was promenading with one of the officers. He told me afterwards that he stayed "aft" as long as he could *that day*.—It

was the third matinée I think, when Mr Dillingham
asked if he might introduce him. He is a midship-
man, & though I thought he was only twenty, he
told me he was twenty-two. Still he seemed like a
boy to me, & I know I am the first person he ever
was interested in; I could hardly believe that he had
never before attended one of the matinées, or went
to any of the hops, which are given every Saturday
at the "naval academy." Young men are so diffirent,
some of them run after girls from the time they are
in petticoats, & instinctively know what to do & say,
when they are with them. And others like Jay Pierrepont, Mr Little, or Nick Devereux, dont care anything about them, till some one rouses them. I rather
like the indiffirent ones, & several of the kind are
my very particular friends. Mr Berry is an exceedingly handsome fellow, but so undeveloped in some
things still he talks very well, & I know he liked me
*very* much. He gave me his photograph, and a
sil      , & the sixth button on the left side of his
coat, & a "Franklin ribbon" to say nothing of an
exquisite boquet of white camilias. He was awfully
cut up about going off, but his Sister is in Rome, &
as he had not seen her for two years, he had asked
for three weeks leave. (I think flirting is a contemptable thing, & I wont do it.) He spent his last evening
here, & looked as handsome as a picture. he did not

like to say good bye either. On Friday, we were en-
vited to a very swell dejeuner on the Franklin. We
went down at ten o'clock, & first they had "general
quarters," which is a real naval battle, without the
fire & smoke. I shall always feel as if I had been in
action now. Capt Parker had given Mr Burroughs
a letter to write to "the honorable secretary of the
navy" which Mr Burroughs thought a great bore.
So whenever capt Parker went below, or disappeared
for a moment, Mr Burroughs would race out of the
cabin, & we would have a little chat; but whenever
Capt Parker hove in sight he would be back in his
place & writing in the most proper manner. The
consequence was, that the letter to the honorable
secretary of the navy, did not progress very rapidly,
in fact he made a fine mess of it, & even directed it
to the wrong man.—-The breakfast party consisted
of, General Sheridan, Gen. Forsyth Admiral Boggs,
Capt.s Parker & Howell, the Fellows'es, Mr Folger,
Boggs, Housel, & Thackery, who compose the staff.
It was a very swell breakfast, & I was frightfully
bored.—We saw a great deal of General Sheridan
while he was here; he used to drive with us in the
afternoons, & then come up & spend the evening. He
was equally devoted to Sister & I, & we liked him
very much. He & Bismarck are great friends: he was
at Sedan & with the headquarters of the Prussian

army during their entire march to Paris. He says the prince royale, & his bretheren are mere figure-heads; it is there subordinates that do all the work.—A lady told Mamma that it was generally believed, that Sister is engaged to General Sheridan, & I to Mr Francia.—

### MARCH 18TH

WE ARE on the eve of our departure for Naples. The Franklin has gone; Mr Berry & Mr Little both spent their last evenings here. Mr Little (who never likes any one, or goes anywhere if he can help it) has made between sixteen & nineteen evening calls here; he cooly appropriated eleven of his cards which he found in the card basket. He is entirely diffirent from any one else, & a very nice fellow, & he has qualities which I have never seen united in any one else.—In the first place he is very handsome; & very good; & then he is very jolly, very accomplished, very refined, & very fastidious.—We have been on two very jolly parties to Monaco, given by Mrs Shaw; & consisting of Miss Shaw, & her two admirers, Mason & Rogers, Mr Schemmerhor, Mr Burroughs, Sister & I. We enjoyed ourselves immensely, & also at a picnic given by Mason, with the same people, & Mr Hunker & Miss Williamson in addition. Mr Berry got back from his three weeks leave on Sunday morning, & Sunday evening as I was sitting alone in the salon, the door opens & in walks Mr Berry; he did not look *very sorry* to shake hands again.—With the Francia's we have certainly had a most curious time; we have seen them almost every day for six months, & fortunately we part good friends all around, without any unpleasantness on either side. I really think Mrs Francia is fond of me, & as for Sissy, she is my devoted friend; in fact she talks to me very much as Minnie does.—

### NAPLES MARCH

WE HAD a levee of farewells, the day & evening before we left Nice; at about eight P. M. Piquée made his appearance, followed almost instantly by Burroughs. Francia has never dared to call *once*, since his first visits, when he was sent away repeatedly, & so he looked like a cat in a strange garret when he came in.—The last time I saw him I had made a dissertation on the horror of men, who wore any color about their clothes; & so he came dressed in the blackest black, & looking more foreign, feindish, & disgusting than ever. His manners, at least as far as I am concerned have vastly improved, & he is positively afraid of me now. Of course he must see my water-colors, & praise them up to the proper pitch, & call himself an artist, & me an artist, etc. etc. He finally departed about half past nine, & then

I talked to Mr Burroughs till eleven, & he departed, though he said, he did not intend it to be "good bye" for good, by any means.—I like Nice immensely, & I owe a great deal to it, for I was very sick and miserable when we came down from Vevey, & every one tells me how very much better I look. Indeed I really am beginning to believe that I am getting well; The faint turns & chills that I used to have every day, have nearly disappeared, & I can walk twenty minutes without being exhausted, though it has taken a year & a half of the most faithful, constant & devoted care from Sister & Mamma, to get me to where I am now. Once in a while, I have a faint speck of color in my countenance, & those immense black circles under my eyes are not so fearfully prominent. But I still have to be so careful, the slightest neglect in the matter of food for instance, a cup less of beef tea, a smaller dinner, or an hour's less sleep, will put me all back. Sometimes I can not believe that I am the same girl that I used to be before this strange, & incomprehensible illness; I used to dance so hard, & play croquet four hours at a time, & walk, & skate, & read, read, read, & now every one says the youngest Miss Newberry "is *so* delicate"; & three years ago, it was always, "oh how tall you are for your age," quite enormous" so fat, so strong, etc. etc. At any rate I am much

better looking than I was before I was sick which is
a great comfort.

NAPLES APRIL 3RD
HOTEL DE RUSSIE

WE CAME through from Nice by boat direct, &
reached here a week ago Friday. On Saturday morning Mr Little, & Mr Hunker, called, & then went with
us to the Opera to hear Don Carlos.—Sunday Mr
Berry came, up, & Mr Little dined with us.—Monday Little & Hunker took us in one of the Franklin
boats to visit the "Lord Warden" a British Iron-
clad; we were most hospitably entertained, & the
ship was splendid. Teusday Capt Parker came to
dinner, & we went to the opera, where Mr Rogers &
Mr Little speedily discovered us—Wednesday Mr
Berry called, & stayed to dinner. Thursday Mr
Little went with us to hear "La Juive", & Mr Berry
came up in our box. Friday evening Mr Little
called. Saturday was the last of the Franklins stay,
& we did a variety of things. An expedition to Capri
was proposed, & fell through. Very much disappointed Sister & I started out for a ride; on the
stairs we meet Mr Little, who does not refuse to ac-
company us. We go up the Toledo, & then meander
among the coral shops; on our way back to the hotel,
behold Mr Folger, who stops the carriage, & says he
has brought the "steam launch", & we must take a

sail. This proposition is backed by Mr Berry in
his midshipmans jacket, who is supposed to be "on
watch", but has been some how misteriously relieved. Mamma must now entertain the Admiral,
(who is an old horror) & so Sister & I go off in the
Launch; it is a perfect day with a nice little breeze,
& the Launch rolls & tosses delightfully; the men
smoke, & we steam nearly to Baïe, Mr Berry is
rather blue with the prospect of sailing next day, but
nevertheless it is all great fun; on our way back, we
pass the Franklin, when suddenly the band strikes
up, & Capt Parker appears on the poop, & beckons
us on board. Sister says "shall we?" & I answer
"yes of course" so up we go, to have a last look at
her.—Mr Berry insists that I shall dance a waltz
with him, so we take a turn on the gun-deck, while
the band plays my favorite, "Soldaten Lieder." I
am awfully sorry to bid the "Franklin" good-bye,
& to think that our "jolly times" are all over; I know
the navy so well now, that I almost feel as if I belonged to it. But all nice things in this world do
come to end, & perhaps after all, we should not
enjoy them as much, if we thought they would last
for ever. So we shake hands with the Captin, & any
stray officers that happen to be about, & go over the
side of the ship for the last time.—In the evening,
as soon as he got off watch, Mr Berry came up, &

settled into a big chair on one side of the fire place, & then Mr Little came a few minutes afterwards, & sat down in another. It was horrid having them both there, because each wished the other a thousand miles away, & men are so disagreeable in such cases, they will not converse together, & each expects one's undived attention, Sister talked to Mr Hunker, & Mamma was not there.—Mr Berry was down in the dumps, & hardly spoke, while Mr Little ignored their departure entirely, & talked faster than ever. I was utterly worn out with all I had been doing during the day, but of course I could not leave. Finally Mr Berry with a deep sigh got up to go, & after saying good bye, vanished through the doorway. Mr Little much relieved took another chair, & we had some more random conversation. But he is so queer, not a word about his going, not the slightest allusion to our ever meeting again; & yet for three months I have seen him constantly, & he has seized every opportunity of meeting. And if I had seen as much of any ordinary young man, as I have of him, I should consider that he had been very attentive; but Mr Little never goes any where, or likes anybody, & he is most extraordinary in that respect; every where he goes he is noticed, & spoken of, & universally admired by men & women. But on him people do not seem to produce any effect. Now the Ogden girls used to rave about him, & I could hardly make him acknowledge their existance; he did not seem ever to have thought or know anything about them.——Young ladies did not seem to interest him atall, & Mr Hunker says he nevers likes any one; & yet there is not the slightest affectation on his part, not a bit. So altogether I am rather proud of having him for my friend, especially as I have never done the slightest thing to attract his attention.——I never but once asked him to come into our rooms, & I had twenty-three of his cards. I never went to see Mrs Little but three or four times the whole winter, though I often wanted to. It is one thing for a person to have a young man around, who devotes himself to a pretty girl every where he goes, & quite another to have a friend like Mr Little, & I esteem it a great compliment.——For a long time I could not tell, whether he liked me any better after a dozen visits, than he did in the beginning. But twords the end I could see a very decided diffirence; he liked "Hyperion" & "Miss Proctor" so much & appreciated them I think; & on all matters of taste we agreed exactely.——He is still extremely shy, that is to say for a man of his age, & altogether a very nice queer, original individual. We had great fun the three nights we went to the opera; the first time we heard Don Carlos, we talked the whole time, & both pro-

nounced the opera heavy, with no music in it. But
the first half, of the second time, he was in the pit;
& we both listened, & found there was a great deal.
—Mr Little never paid compliments, but he *did*
complimentary things.—I am most absurdly fastidious about gentlemens dress, & I once in Nice, when
he was in the room, said I thought the officers looked
infinitely better in their uniforms, & that I liked
them so much better. He has never been to see me
without his uniform, since that day. And yet that
last evening, he said nothing about his going off,
up to the last minute. Finally I said quietly, "I hope
Mr Little if you are any where around where we
are next Summer, that you will look us up? He
laughed, & answered emphatically, "I *certainly*
shall."—They staid till I was at the last gasp, &
then Mr Little & I, shook hands, & he showed himself out, looking as handsome as a picture, &, (but
I wont say just a little pale & sorry) why should he?
- - Next morning the Franklin sailed away, & when
we sat down to breakfast she was out of sight.—It
is curious to note the facility with which people forget each other. Now when I am with people I like,
we enjoy ourselves, & I like them so very much; &
I think, "oh, dear, when we go away, how sorry I
shall be," but we go away, & I imagine that I feel
very bad, & somebody else comes along, & then

there is the same story right over again. And then
there are only a few, that you care ever to see again.
I am not able to do much sight seeing, & I missed a
great deal, that I wanted to see, but this is one of
the small trials, many of which I have to endure so
many besides my illness. There were some full
lengths by Vandyke & Reubenns, & Guido's St
Sebastian in the Brignoli Palace at Genoa, that I
enjoyed more than anything I have seen here, except the Psyche, which is the first bit of marble,
that ever gave me any real satisfaction. I feel so
sorry to loose, Sorrento, Pompeii, & Capri, but I
have felt so ill the last few days that we dare not stay
in this malaria country any longer.


BATHS OF LUCCA, MAY 10TH

I HAVE seen Rome! & was only allowed to remain
two days, was there ever anything more barbarous?
Our arrival was not propitious; utterly exhausted
by the journey from Naples, I barely reached our
rooms in the hotel de Russie, before one of my terrible fainting fits came on.—I had an awful time,
& Mamma & Sister, were very much alarmed. The
next day, I managed to get dressed, & though I had
to be very careful, & drink tea by the wholesale, I
was able to go about in a carriage. The first thing
we saw was Saint Peters. It far surpassed my ex-

pectations, & the beauty & harmony of the whole
impressed me greatly. Pauvre moi! I was only allowed a half an hour, to take it all in. (Half an
hour, for Michael Angelo's chef d'œuvre.) It was
holy-week, & the "Vatican," & principal galleries
were closed, another disappointment added to the
many. But I did see *the* "Cenci." If I had been ex-
pecting to see my dearest friend I should not have
been as excited; & when we finally reached the Bar-
barini Palace, & were ushered into the Cenci's
presence, I found to my inexpressible disappointment that her eyes were - - - brown. And I hate brown
eyes!! It is quite true that there is something about
the original, that the copiests can not catch; some
subtle fascination peculiar to itself; I liked it immensely, but it was far less beautiful than I expected. We visited the Coliseum, & dug up a "live
ruin" in the shape of Mr G. W. Wurtz.—But Rome
was so much smaller, lighter, & cleaner than I expected. The houses were not as tall, nor the streets
half as narrow as I expected; indeed Genoa was
much more as I thought Rome would be. Still I liked
it, & was sorry enough to come away so soon. We
were three weeks in Florence; the first week we
were all sick, & the last week I ran down steadily,
& have continued to do so. Mr Wurtz the last individual on the tapis, did his best to make himself

agreeable to my honorable Sister, by calling twice
a day, & sending huge baskets of flowers. I dislike
him, as I generally dislike Sisters beaux! Guido's
Cleopatra in the Pitti, is simply superb! there was
a head of Rhembrandt by himself that I liked very
much, & several other things.

BADEN BANDEN
JUNE 16TH
THE DAY OF THE GRAND
ENTREE INTO BERLIN

I FIND to my sorrow, that I have not written in my
journal since I was in Lucca, but I was so miserable
there, & so wretchedly sick during the journey to
Geneva, that writing has been out of the question.—
We were three days at Bologna where I had a most
awful sick head-ache (frightful) by way of variety.
The last morning I managed to see "the Saint Ce-
celia". It *was* beautiful! There were two or three
splendid Guidos in the gallery.—Bologna is a queer
old place, full of real "genre" pictures, & I liked it
very much.—Turin our next stopping place, seemed
like a miniature Paris, but it was far too new &
clean to be picturesque.—We stopped all night at
Suza, & then oh! misery left at eight the next morning to cross the Mont Cenis.—It was very extraordinary to feel oneself going in & out, backwards &
forwards, up & down, round & round the mountain

at the most tremendous speed, & if I had not suffered so, I should have enjoyed it very much. *The*
scenery was magnificent, & I am very glad we went
over the mountain, for the railroad is to be taken
down as soon as the great Mont Cenis tunnel is completed.—Arrived on the other side we hoped to go
on to Chamberie to spend the night, which was only
three hours distant but I was at the very last ebb,
nearly fainting with a seperate ache in every limb,
& nothing could have moved me another inch. So
we were obliged to stop where we were, & sleep in
the nastiest wayside-inn, with the beasts of the field
below us.—I have suffered a great deal since I have
been sick but never more than during this last trip.
—The journey to Geneva was fearful also! Once
there I rallied again; we sent for the celebrated Dr
Binet, whom we liked very much.—He agreed with
Dr Grey whom I saw in Utica, in what he said
about my illness. He told me to sleep twenty-five
hours out of the twenty-four if I could! He said
first that I had developed bodily & mentally much to
fast & now I have to make up for it, by perfect quiet
of mind & body. I am not allowed to read anything
serious, or have any kind of a lesson. I think think
the whole time & that I cant help; I wanted to know
German as well as I know French, which could only
be done by my going to school in Dresden; but they

say I musn't think of such a thing as taxing my
brain any more, & that this lazy, idle stupid, dull
life is the only thing for me. As soon as I begin to
fail in one place we must leave it & go to another.—
I can draw & paint though when ever I have a good
day, & no one knows the pleasure it gives me. I
learnt a great deal from Mon. Vigna last Winter
& he told me, (& he is a *very severe* critic,) that he
was certain that I possed all the needful qualities
to be an artist, & a *real* one.—But of course to be
one I must go through a hard & thorough course of
study.—I never felt so happy in my life as when
he said so. If I were obliged to earn my living, I
might make a name for myself that would last, but
situated as I am, it is more than likely that I shall
live a comfortable life, & die & be forgotten.—But
no matter what I do, my own dear Papa, will never
know it, & he would have cared so much.—I re-
visited Mlle Pelet, & found them all looking just the
same; there is no one I respect & admire as I do
Mlle Steiner, she is an angel on earth. Her piety is
so real, unafected, & sincere, & yet she is so ready
to enjoy anything that comes in her way, & sympa-
thizes so heartily with everything that interests
others.—My little cousin Minnie, is now larger than
I, & fifteen years old; health & freshness, most
caracterize her looks at present, & she is most ab-

surdly unsophisticated in her ideas.—She develops
in the slowest possible manner, it seems to me as if
she never would begin to be "grown up."—

Just for fun I am going to write out a discription
of my Summer outfit, fashions change so, that it will
be quite curious to read it over in a year or two.

Two linen dresses, worn over black silk petticoats,
one embroidered in black, the other white
batiste.—

White overdress, (nansook) trimmed with "bands-
de-saxe".—

White cachemere, (over blue silk petticoat,)
trimmed with cluny; neck cut square.—

Calico, trimmed with magenta, very pretty.

Black glace, silk costume, ouvert en coeur, over-
skirt trimmed with heavy fringe.—

Pink muslin, made with white organdie.—

White spotted muslin, flounces of organdie, embroidered, pink bows, & sash.—

Black & white silk, trimmed with white cluny &
black lace, elegant corsage, cut open to match.—

Black hussar jacket, braided.—

Black sailor hat.—

Jaunty leghorn hat, brown velvet, & pink rose;
awfully pretty.*—

*Believed to be the hat worn as pictured in the frontispiece.—*Ed.*

Cravates of crèpe de chine, with tasels, all delicate
colors.—

White silk, cane, parasol.—

Blue faille silk, of a lovely French blue, all trimmed
with delicate blue lace.—A tall white chip hat,
very high like a helmet, with blue to match, blue
feathers, & two little parrorts wings very chic.

Pink silk, with white gaze de chamberie over-dress;
the tunic long, garni de fringe, & a most exquisite waist, overt en coeur.

A walking dress of some curious indian stuff, light
brown, with fringe, over a magnificent, cerise
faille petticoat.—These last three have just arrived from Paris & were sent by "Pingat", & of
course are as stunning as they can be.—Then
Julie Tillons sent us another box, in which for
me there were two white nansook dresses, & a
white muslin over dress, trimmed with blue ribbon under the puffings. A white muslin trimd
with valenciennes, over pink silk, & a stunning
white piquée, made with a very long over skirt,
& lots of insertion & "bandes de saxe".—

A tall white hat with white feathers.—


All the dresses are made with flounced under-
skirts, & over dresses very much looped in the back.
Broad sashes, & half flowing sleeves, & most of the

waists "overt en coeur". All are short costumes no one wears long dresses now, except at grand balls.—

### JULY 11TH

LAST Wednesday my friend Mr. Burroughs made his appearance,—he has shaved off his side-whiskers & looks much better & broader.—He is as jolly & amusing as possible; but ever since he sent me that superb boquet last Winter, with eighty-two camilias in it, my Sister has taken to bothering me.—Some of the people in Nice used to suppose he was attentive to Hattie Warren because he used to walk on the Promenade with her, & since I left Nice several people have acquainted me with the fact; of course I always say "oh yes" though inwardly I am convulsed. The fair Hattie has been in a great state (about his coming) - - - The first two weeks here it poured the whole time, & it was awfully slow. Mrs Little was my only resource, & I went to see her every day or two.—She manages to have a pretty easy time take it all together;—she is very amusing & I like her immensely.

### JULY 12TH

THE Ogdens have come, & are a great help. They are in splendid condition, & Maggie is as handsome as ever. I think I am slightly insane on the subject

of beauty.—No matter how much I dislike an individual, I nevertheless enjoy their good-looks if
they have any.   And as for handsome women in
general, no man can admire them more than I do.—
I never look at my own Mother even, without con-
sidering how she looks! I couldn't marry an ugly
man, his looks would distress me so; & if he was
very handsome I should admire him all day long.—

MONDAY JULY 17TH

THIS morning Minnie (who has been here several
days,) & I took a walk.—We meandered about
among the shops, & presently Mr Burroughs made
his appearance.—When we get together we talk a
perfect stream, & laugh the whole time; he is very
funny & he makes me funny.—We then prolonged
our walk as far as the Ogdens, & I took him up
to see them—We found Maggie & Mamie looking
fresh & fair, & it was awfully nice & cool.—They
gave us wine & sirup, & we laughed & talked non-
sense for about an hour & a half, in their parlor.—
Then we started home again; & dodged about to
keep out of the sun, for I have no desire to have a
second sun-stroke.—We go over to the Kursaal in
the evenings now & listen to the music. We sit down
or promenade as the case may be; the other night
we were all seated together, the Clapps, the Ogdens,

Hooker Hammersly, Mr Frank Ogden, Mr Burroughs, all the beaux that are here in fact:—Mamie
her brother & I, all drove up & sketched the "Alten
Schloss" last week; I like this place ever so much.
Hooker H. has been here ten days, & is decidely
attentive to Sister.—They take walks & he performs
generally. His surroundings are very well, but he
is not the man for My Sister by a long short.—

### FRIDAY. JULY 21ST

I AM afraid to write that I am better for fear I shall
be sick again, but I have had four such good
weeks.—I am so thankful, & to feel well is really
such happiness, independant of all the nice time
we are having.—Every-one congratulates me on my
improved appearance, which is very refreshing. The
Clapps leave to-day; they have been here a week,
& Minnie has enjoyed her visit immensely. She is
going to school in Dresden now, & I would willing
give up all my fine clothes, young-lady-hood &
beaux, to go with her this Winter & learn German.
Teusday, Mrs Clapp, Minnie, Mr Burroughs & I,
went up to the new Schloss; we went all over it,
saw the pictures of all the grand Dukes of Baden,
& the dungeons which are superb. Mamie Ogden,
& Sissy Francia went with me to sketch, which was
great fun. Mr B. & I spent the evening with Mrs

Little, & played with Rags. Last night H. H. & H. B. came up & escorted us over to the Kuhrsaal; we sat on the piazza & had six or seven men to talk to us, Mr Kane, Higginson, Frank Ogden, Joe Francia, etc, to the great disgust of the Warrens who had no one.—

### TEUSDAY. JULY 25

LAST night Mr Kane dined with us, & then we went over & looked on at the ball. I have seen him four days running now, & he is slightly demonstrative; we are engaged to dance a German together next winter at Nice.—Mr Burroughs, I see about twice a day; I know him so very well now, but I have to be so very careful for he would be serious, if I allowed him, & that I dont wish him to be.—Last night we went over to hear Strauss; he played inside the Kursaal, & the large hall was so full that we could not get inside. So we went into another room & while Sister & H. H. remained on the sofa, Mr Kane & Mr Burroughs escorted me about, one on each side like a body-guard.—We watched the "rouge et noir" & then the roulette, & finally we managed to squeeze into the concert-room & hear & see Strauss, who acted like a monkey.—And then those two youths sat on the same stool, while they talked to me, & they nearly fell off; though they tried their best to keep on, & altogether we had great fun & it

was very absurd. This afternoon Piquée called
but I would not see him.—

### THURSDAY. JULY 27TH

LAST night Mr Burroughs sent up his card, & I never
dreaming that he was going away sent word I could
not see him.—This morning he sent up another card
saying he was going right off & hoped he might say
good bye.—I have had Mr Kane the last few days,
& have hardly seen Mr Burroughs, & it was too provoking. He came in looking as handsome as possible, in the loveliest little brown jacket; he at first
looked very "chipper" & evidently had determined
not to look the least bit blue; but his cheerfulness
did not last very long; poor fellow, I am sure I
am not conceited in thinking he really likes me very
much; but he said I always snubbed him once an
hour, & indeed I did say very sharp things; but the
trouble has been that Sister dislikes him, & we have
never even invited him once to dinner in all the time
I have known him.—He knew of course and has
known from the beginning that I cared no more for
him than for Mr Little or Mr Berry, & I think he
concluded it would be safer for him to go right off.
He is very sensitive & doesn't require much to make
him understand! So he sat on one chair & I on
another, & we both talked about indiffirent matters

as people always do. He acted just like a woman, in
trying to appear indiffirent, & he did not betray the
slightest feeling either by word or action, except
once when the tears came into his eyes.—He thought
I did not see them but I did.—I never liked him
as much as when I knew he was going off, but then
that is always the way,—when they run after me I
don't care for them, but if they stay away I want to
see them. I hope I am not a flirt & yet sometimes I believe I am.—I never saw a *young* man before that
understood women as well as he does.—We have had
such awfully nice times together, at Monaco, at the
matinées, on various expeditions, & now here.—
He was introduced to me in January, & we were
great friends directly.—But it was an odd coincidence, that Mr Little should have arrived last night
& escorted Mr Burroughs to the depot this morning.
First I bid one good bye & then in about two hours
the other appeared. Such is life! Heigh oh!—

### AUGUST 3RD 1871
### THURSDAY

I NEVER enjoyed myself more that I have during the
last four weeks; in the first place I have felt so well,
& then it has been so jolly.—Sister has been fully
occupied, & I always enjoy myself so much more
when she is thinking about something else.—Mr

Burroughs was here over two weeks, & entirely devoted to me; the Sunday before he left Mr Kane
called, & then after that I saw him all the time, until
he went off to Homburg. Thursday Mr Burroughs
left & then Mr Little came; he had invested in a grey
suit, & with a straw hat, pearl colored kids & a rose
in his button-hole, he looked exceedingly well. He
dined with us on Friday, & Sat. morn. Sister & I,
with Mr Hammersly, & Mr Little, drove out to "La
Favourite" a most curious chateau; in one room
there are more than forty portraits of the same
woman; there is also a great deal of curious china,
with dishes for the table made to represent the vegi-
tables, or birds they were intended to hold.—There
was one room lined with slabs of Florentine mosaic,
etc, & then by way of contrast there was a kind of
chapelle expiatoire, in which she did penance all
alone by herself, for forty days every year.—That
evening Mr Little was engaged by the Warrens to
dine with them, & so I went over to the Kurhsaal ex-
pecting to have rather a stupid time, when who
should rush up but Mr Kane, whom I did not expect
to see for a month.—First thing he did was to tell
me he had come back to see me, & then he was sorry
he had said it, & began to invent five hundred diffirent excuses for his appearance.—He has the
polish given by an English education, with all an

Americans energy.—I always metion the people I like in here, but never a word about all the youths I gently dismiss.—On Sunday Mr Kane called again, & on Monday the whole three spent the morning with us, & when my two friends had departed, Mr Hammersly must needs make a fool of himself, & ask Sister to marry him.—He was both astonished & mortified, when she declined the honor; that evening there was to be a ball, & Strauss the magnificent was to lead his own waltzes.—Poor Hooker escorted Sister, & Mr Kane was with me. the Americans here do not dance at the balls, so we went merely as spectators.—We were early, & found good seats; one after another, every one in Baden appeared; some of the foreign ladies, who are prodigiously ugly, wore long dresses, but generally short costumes were worn. But when Strauss led it was perfectly magnificent; he inspires the band to such a degree, that they play as if under enchantment; Gungle was very fine but Strauss is beyond anything I ever imagined; we got so excited, that Mamie & I nearly screamed, & she kept squeezing my hand & "oh Julia it is too beautiful, I must dance, I cant keep still."— Even Sister who is so cold-blooded & never gets wrought up by anything of the kind, was wildly excited; & when the cotillon began & he led the first waltz, I thought we should go crazy; I never, never heard anything so beautiful.—Several of the rooms were thrown open, so we promenaded about everywhere; Mr Kane devoted himself entirely to me, until Mr Little ousted him.—He had tried & tried to get to me, but as it often happens something was always in the way.—Finally he did succeed, to Mr Kanes great disgust; the cotillon was very amusing though the figures were simply inane, they fished at eachother, & shot hearts with bows & arrows; I have heard people expaciate in the most absurd manner about the good looks of the German officers, there were plenty there that night, & they all had red faces & tow colored hair.—The Prussian uniform, black with red facings is hidious! the honorable Miss Loftus, considered a beauty in England, sat in front of me; for an honorable damsel her hair was exceedingly frowzy.—Hattie Warren was whirling about with a very common young man, & poor Mary Ida looked as stupid as ever.—We went home in a rapturous state, after a never to be forgotten evening, & my brain played waltz after waltz all night long.—Teusday morning Mr Little called again, & he & I & Sister went out & drove in the Lientaal; one of the loveliest drives I know of; that evening Hooker & Mr Kane both dined with us; we had a very jolly dinner, though it was extremely difficult for me to act twords Mr Hammersly, as if I were

unaware of his proposal.—On Wednesday morning
Sister & I were in the reading room, & we had not
been there long when one after another the three
youths appeared; how they all managed to appear
just then is beyond my comprehension.—Mr H. in
a feeble way was nearly frantic en costume de voy-
age, & with the dirtiest pair of gloves I ever had the
pleasure of beholding.—Mr Kane was in a very
funny state; he could not make up his mind, either
to go or stay; Mr Little played "Don Carlos" &
talked alternately, *he* was going at midnight, & no
doubt about it. We talked three hours; bemoaning
in hypocritical terms, our sad fate; for were we not
being deserted, by three gallant knights, who were
leaving us in the most heartless manner; (yes they
were leaving us, but one because he had been re-
jected, & the other because he could n't help himself.
—At 3 P. M. the great Mr Hammersly, retired from
the scene.—I went up stairs & presently Mr Little's
card was brought in & I sent word I was lying down!
At a quarter past four the waiter brought another.
This time he got in. Sister received him, I came in
afterwards; it was very extraordinary his calling
twice in succession that way! He was rather excited,
& did not act just as usual.—He asked if he might
take "Adelaide Proctor" with him to England, & send
it back when he got to Nice. I said he might.—Sister

was on the balcony when he said this. She went out
of the room for about ten minutes; when she came
back she said my cheeks were in a blaze; perhaps
they were! it is such an annoyance to have a pale
transparent skin, the slightest change is instantly
noticed.—I saw him again in the evening, at the
concert; he walked home with us, stayed a moment & then we said good-bye.—At midnight he &
Mr Kane went off together.—

### MONDAY AUGUST 14TH

I HAVE not been well for several days, & only one
particular thing has happened, & that was last
wednesday. I was in bed, feeling wretched, about
three in the afternoon. Sister came into my room to
have her tea, & while she was taking it she related to
me an absurd dream that she had had the night before, about Mr Little & I.—To this tale she added
sundry notes & comments, & waxed eloquent on the
subject of the, to her, quite evident devotion of Mr
Little to me.—I told her she was mistaken, for
though I know he likes me particularly, he never
even had paid me an ordinary compliment, & far
less said anything in the half tender half joking
manner, which my other friends are very apt to
assume.—We argued in this manner for some time,
when (was it accident, coincidence, or fate) a letter

was brought in, with English stamps, & post-marked
Ryde. I was confounded!—Sister has a most nasty
& disagreeable habit of enquiring when ever I get a
letter, as to who it is from; she had caught sight of
the stamps on this one, & of course she gave me no
peace until she had read it.—The letter was from
Mr Little sure enough; his excuse for writing, was
to thank me for letting him take Adelaide Proctor,
which was entirely unnecessary, & to announce what
his Mother had already told me, that he was "going
to America with the ship, but coming back immediately on a six months leave,"—when he "hoped
to have the pleasure of seeing me, & obtain my par-
don for his temerity in writing."—Well of course
Sister was perfectly furious; she stormed away for
about an hour, in high tragedy style.—"Wasn't this
a conformation of just what she had been telling
me? was there ever anything so preposterous as his
writing that letter, so totally unnecessary! so absurd.
Had n't she told me it would be so? had n't she for-
seen it all? (So she had for about a week.) "And
then the *idea* of his coming out again when he had
n't been home for five years, & his Mothers buisiness
affairs were in such an unsetteled state! Of course
he was coming out to see me, there was no doubt
about it; Mrs Little had said she should go to Rome,
& Nice for the Winter, & Mr Little has already spent

four Winters in Nice, & hates it accordingly.—What other reason could there be for his going there? And then the idea of infant of my age, only seventeen, having such performances! And so she went till I was perfectly exhausted.—

I HAVE not been to see Mrs Little since before Mr Little came, nearly four weeks, & as I used to go every two days, my absence is too marked not to be speculated upon, & of course she is furious.—I hate to make her angry, but it is the only way in which I can let her see that if her son is coming over on my account,—he had much better stay in America.— Ideed she ought to be very much obliged to me, for of course I might pretend I knew nothing about it, act just as usual, & have the pleasure & satisfaction of his being devoted to me all next Winter.—But it worries me so; He is such a splendid fellow, & we have been such good friends, & I admire & esteem him so much, & I was so sure that he was so constitutionally indiffirent to girls, & that with him at least I might have a solid friendship, without any sentiment just as if we were two men; & now to have it all spoiled. I dont believe that the young men now a days really care much about any-one, but with him it is diffirent for he never has had even the most

passing fancy for any one, & after all he is twenty-
four years old & not a baby. And I should feel
awfully if he should get to care about me really.—I
have never snubbed him, because he has never given
me a chance, & until that letter came, I never dreamt
or believed that there was anything on his side.—
Why the last night, though he knew he was going
off, he never even asked me to walk up & down,
never said he was sorry to go, never said a thing in
his whole life to me, that implied any thing particular. Of course I saw he was diffirent than when I
first knew him, but his coming to see me all the time,
is just what he has always done, & altogether I am
dreadfully perplexed; I told Sister once that I was
quite sure, that if we were thrown together in the
same neighborhood for ten years that at the end of
that time he would perhaps care for me, & that is
just what I thought about it. I think he is certainly
the queerest young man I ever saw, & I am sure no
one else would behave in the same way.—But then
he is so handsome & so good, & I consider it such a
compliment his liking me atall.—And then I may
never see him again, & it is altogether horrid.—We
went to the opera & heard trovatore very badly sung,
Krauss the same prima-donna that was in Naples.—

List of people we know, here at
Baden this Summer

| | |
|---|---|
| Warrens.— | Francias. |
| Phoenix.— | Ogdens.— |
| Osborns.— | Clapps.— |
| Winthropes.— | Pells.— |
| Hammersly. | Burroughs.— |
| Suares.— | Kanes.— |
| Mr Little.— | Coxes. |
| Prescott. | Fish. |
| Fields, | Princesse Brancacio |
| Kane. | Mrs Little |
| Demming | Mrs M. O. Roberts |
| Wilcoxon. | Miss Niles. |
| Higginson. | Conte de Sessee |
| J. A. Grey. | Ct. Corrie. |
| Kings.— | Lawrences.— |
| McCaggs. | |

### SUNDAY AUGUST 27TH

OF COURSE having been well one month, I have been
poorly again, & so we are off de nouveau! This is
the loveliest place, & I've had such a good time, &
I'm so sorry to go. It suits me exactly; the lazy life,
the black forest, the old castles, the music all day
long, enfin everything. The only places I like any-
where are, Chicago, St Augustine, Richfield—
Springs, Nice, & Baden-Baden, & New York pretty
well.—Hamilton Fish, Jr. has been here a few days,
he seemed to be a nice youth.—This afternoon we
sat in the Alley, & talked to the Brancacios, the

Prince is a queer being. This afternoon I buckled on
my armour & went to say fare-well to Mrs Little.—
She met Mamma in the street the other day, stopped
her, wanted to know why she had n't been to see her,
& burst into tears, & said she knew very well *why*
she had n't been to see her. Mrs Warren was already
in her room when I went up this afternoon, & fortunately Mrs L. was in a good humour.

Mrs. L. My darling child I'm so glad to see you.

"I have come Mrs Little to make my *"PPC"*.

Are you really going? etc etc.

Well *I* have about decided to go to America in
October, I am in dispair about it. I'm so seasick,
but I've written to Willie & he's written to me, & I
think it is better for his futur prospects, & his *present* prospects for him to go.

(Looking straight at her steadily) I'm sure I
dont see *why* Mr Little should wish to come back to
Europe. I should think he would like to stay in his
own country. (I'm sure there is nothing I could have
said more decisive than that.—) Mrs L. discon-
certed said she thought so too. Something was said
about early marriages & I remarked that a girl only
18 or 19 could n't know her own mind, & it was perfectly absurd for girls to be married so *young,* & so
we talked for some time.

LUCERNE. AUGUST 31ST

WE LEFT Baden on Monday. The Ogdens came to say good-bye & while they were there, in came Mrs Little, very much excited; she asked Sister to come into another room, because she had something very particular to say to her. When they were alone, she said she *must* know why we were all so diffirent, Sister need n't deny it; she knew there was something the matter; we had n't been to see her, & we had never once mentioned Mr Little's name since he left, which was very unatural, when we had been such great friends, & what *had* he done? Sister said there was nothing, but she insisted, & said there must be something, & cried, & cried till finally Sister did what she had no right to do, she told her Mr Little had written me a letter, & as I was not accustomed to receiving letters from gentlemen we did not like it. —And that I was very young to young to think about such things etc. Sisters account is so very confused that I can only understand the general drift & a few detached sentances. Mrs L. told her that she had had a "talk in the dark" with him before he left, & he said he "liked me much better than any girl he had ever seen, & that I was the only woman he would ever care to pass his life with, that he did n't think he was *in love* with me now, but that he should be if he saw any more of me, that if I was a poor girl it might do, but under the circumstances it would be much better for him to go away & never see me again.—He said he did n't think I cared for him now, but that perhaps I might! I think it was dreadful in his Mother to tell Sister all this, told to her of course in the strictest confidence, & what I have no right to know. I'm sure I dont know what Sister said to her, it was certainly a most extraordinary conversation. She was evidently tormented to know if her son had committed himself; & among other things she said he was a perfect child & so they went on.—Mrs Little almost swore that she would never let him know that she knows about the letter, & she thanked Sister for relieving her mind, over & over again & finally she came in & kissed me good bye, the tears streaming down her face, & in her confusion kissed the two Ogdens also. I never saw such a woman, she acts entirely on impulse, & who but her would ever have said such things, & yet she is very nice & I like her very much.—I know I have done what is right; by staying away & being horrid to Mrs Little I have made her understand, that if he intended to get six months leave on my account, he had much better not. Even without directly encouraging him, I might have remained passive & let things take there course, he would have come over, & neither he nor his mother could have blamed me

for it; as before that letter he had never made the
slightest demonstration. I have been an angel for
once in my life, & probably shall be sorry for it.—
Sister was certainly not justified in telling her about
the letter & it was a great breach of confidence on her
part, though she does not seem to think so.—

Le temps emporte sur son aile,
Et le printemps et l'hirondelle,
La vie, et les jours perdus;
Tout s'en va comme la fumée,
Et moi qui vous ait tant aimée,
Et toi, qui t'en souviens plus.

There is something about that verse that haunts
me, & keeps buzzing in my brain all day long; how
tired I do get of thinking perpetually, I wish I could
stop.—And at night when I am *so* tired, & so sleepy,
my brain begins to work, & goes harder than at any
other time.—I think about every body I know, about
all my particular friends, about every thing that is
going on, & puzzle over religion, education, & the
whys & "wherefors", until I feel perfectly frantic; to
go to bed early, & lie awake four or five hours every
night is dreadful.—Before I was sick I never used
to dream, but now I do so very often; I dont see why
we should dream atall, it does us no good what
ever.—I envy people who believe in dreams, visions,

ghosts, omens, & presentiments, it must afford them
so much amusement. I never could make myself believe anything; I never was afraid of the dark, &
have always enjoyed breaking looking-glasses, because the servants are always in such a state.—As
for ghosts, I would go any-where alone to meet one,
at midnight or any other time, provided I could be
positively certain, that I should not meet any *live
men*, for I *am* afraid of them.—I think it is very
odd, that girls in New York should be allowed to
walk in any part of the city alone, because even if
the ordinary street "canaille" do not annoy them,
there is always the possibility that a drunken man
may insult them.—I have been reading Wordsworth,
& trying to like him, but I dont! Nor Burns or Shelley either. But Coleridge's Ancient Mariner is
simply superb, & it gives me the same curious uneasy feeling that Poes Raven does.—

LUCERNE HOTEL SCHWEIZERHOF
FRIDAY. SEPTEMBER 8TH
IN THE READING ROOM

SISTER & Mamma have gone up the Rhigi & I am
left to chaperone myself until seven this evening.—
How I hate travelling in Europe, & above all travelling in Switzerland. I began hating it when I had
reached the advanced age of six, & now that I am

seventeen I continue in the same frame of mind.—I
believe I am fated like the "Wandering Jew" to be
on a perpetual journey, & I do wish it would come
to an end.—If we settle down in a place as we did
at Baden & at Nice, I like it well enough, & enjoy
myself extremely, but such intervals like oasis in
the desert are extremely rare, & there are months &
months, composed of dreary days, spent in nasty
cars, or shut up in rooms at a hotel.—If I were perfectly well, & could walk, go sight seeing, ride horse-
back, & sketch as much as I want to, it might be en-
durable, but as it is now, I cant bear it.—Now here
is a specimen of it.—We arrived here ten days ago;
the hotel overflowing! six telegrammes procured us
a comfortable salon & two bed-rooms, but *very
sunny*.—Can we change for a cooler place? Impossible! hotel is too full! First three days I feel very
well, (family jubilee!) It is absolutely necessary
that we see the lake of Lucerne. Feeble protestations
on my part.—Sister carries the day, & we *see* it.—
See it with a vegance too.—It is roasting when we
start, half way out a tremendous Alpine storm
breaks over the lake.—The people on the narrow
deck are packed like herrings in box, the only cov-
ering, an awning with an oil cloth over it.—Down
comes the rain, harder, heavier every minute.—I
never talk to strangers, but at this moment one of two

rather swell Englishmen, makes a remark. Having shortly before been lectured for the absurdity of always keeping to myself, I answer civilly enough. —Conversation becomes amusing, when suddenly a charming little stream of water, descends from the roof, & makes a puddle in my lap.—Sympathy from the Englishman, but no help for it.—A magnificent streak of forked lightening splits the clouds! My neighbour remarks that "nature's fireworks are finer than mans." I assent, conversation continues, we discuss fifty diffirent subjects, the rain continues also, & the puddle in my lap grows larger. It really was a fearful storm while it lasted; & the danger & novelty were very exciting; & as it was almost dark I could not see the Englishman, & it was quite romantic to be talking to him for an hour or so without seeing his face, so that if we had met next day I should not have known it.—We were very moist when we reached here, & a hot dinner, hot bottle, hot drink, & dry clothes just saved us from getting sick.—So I went from Wednesday until Saturday, three days without being worse, Sunday not so well, & Monday in bed where I have been until now, exhausted with heat, & absolutely miserable. And so it is all the time, besides my original illness which has now lasted two years, I have these small intermittant diseases, which a well person would consider

annoying enough. To go way back when we went
to Florida, I was laid up a week in Richmond with
that horrid nettle rash, & the same in New York.—
And that fearful sun-stroke in Nice that put me back
three months; & then at Rome I was so sick, & we
had such a fearful week at the hotel in Florence, &
then two weeks in Lucca, which I shudder every time
I think of, & then in Baden I had a cold, & a swelled
face, & then all my dreadful faint turns, like the one
between Richmond & Augusta, when we had to get
out at a Southern village called Sumpter, our experiance there only equalled by St Michael, at the
foot of the Mont Cenis.—And all these, except the
faints, seem to have been so unecessary & entirely
unconnected with my illness I dont believe in people
who try to remember everything horrid that happens
to them; I try to forget, & succeed admirably; Sister
says she knows that when once I am well, I will forget, all about how sick I have been; I dont see why
I should try & remember it, though it is certainly
the queerest sickness that any one ever had.—No one
ever sees me except when I feel pretty well & in
good spirits; I make it a point never to bore even
my best friends with any account of my ailments. I
think some of them would be slightly astonished if
they could sometimes see me five minutes after they
have left the house.—How often last winter when

some of those men were there in the evening, I would
laugh for two hours as if I were in perfect health,
entertaining them much more than they entertained
me, & five minutes after they had bowed their shin-
ing uniforms, & smiling selves out of the door, I
would be stretched on the bed, with Mamma rubbing
me, & Sister pouring brandy down my throat.—I
think I am gradually getting over my disease, though
it is a miserably slow affair.—

HOMBOURG LES BAINS.
SEPTEMBER. 15.

WE SPENT three days at Zurich; a nice hotel but a
very stupid place, just like *all* Swiss places.—We
had a curious fellow traveller; a Englishman, very
swell, & superlatively clean. Oh so clean, so clean.
He had on an elegant suit of grey; a delicately
striped red & white shirt, a dark silk scarf, the fleeci-
est of white lambs-wool stockings, & delightful but-
toned boots, exactly like those Colonel Bonaparte
wore.—And then such beautiful hands; small &
shapely, with taper fingers, & almond nails.—A
selfish, pleasure-seeking, over refined, blasé, man
of thirty-nine, whose life is narrowed down to eating, drinking, washing, fishing, shooting & sleeping;
a very highly pampered human animal; he has a
place in Suabia where they catch 250 trout per day;

a fishing hut in Norway, ten miles from any human habitation, where they never wind up their watches, & the sun shines at midnight. He has a house in Paris, & spends part of every Winter in St Petersbourg.—"I think one always feels so cross" he said, "& nasty if one gets up before noon, & then besides the world is not well aired before that time." When he went up the Nile he took an extra boat filled with sheep, & another with hens & chickens; his butter was kept quite fresh in brine, & he had freezing-powders for his champagne.—

SUNDAY SEPTEMBER 17TH

LAST night I heard Patti in Ernani!—I have longed to see her since I was seven years old, & now my desire has been gratified. At first I was disappointed, but then I had expected so very much! She is a small woman, & rather thin; of a Southern or slightly oriental 'type', with a great deal of very black hair, & handsome but peculiar dark eyes, with long lashes, & a pale skin.—I have heard people say that she could not act atall; but that idea is quite bête, for she acts quite as much as a cantatrice needs to. In the highly sentimental parts she is not very demonstrative, & keeps the "tenor" at a sufficiently respectful distance, which is a great improvement upon what one usually sees on the stage.—Her voice was perfectly lovely, & her execution faultless, though I think she might have put a little more soul into it.— Not but what she sang with a great deal of expression, but she did not appear ever to be wholly carried away by the music. Her dresses were gorgeous; in the second act she wore a light blue faille, trimmed with silver lace; in the last a wedding dress of white & gold, with a coronet & vail on the back of her head, which made her look bewitching.—The marquis de Caux sat in the front row, his opera glass raised, watching her attentively during the whole performance, as if he were looking at her for the first time.—The finale she acted with great spirit, & sang it splendidly; she picked up the boquets thrown at her in the most coquettish manner, with the funniest les airs & grimaces, that made us all laugh.—

My favorite books, authors, & poems now are.

*Jane Eyre.*
And all that Charlotte Brontë ever wrote.—
*Adelaide Procter's Poems.*
Miss Thackerys stories.
Vanity Fair.—
Haslitts Essays.—
Marmion.—
Ivanhoe.—

All Byron's decent poems.—
The Ancient Mariner.
*Grey's Elegy.*
Hawthornes house with the seven gables.
*Longfellow's Hyperion.*—
Old Town Folks by Mr Stowe.
King Henry the IV & V.—
Romeo & Juliette.
The Mill on the Floss.
She stoops to Conquer.
A few of Tennysons.
Cooper's Spy.—
A Summer in Leslie Goldwaithe's life.
Ruskins book of beauties.—
Longfellow.
Pickwick Papers.
La Marseillaise.—
Bacon's Essays.
Irving's sketch-book.

Those plays of Shakespear that I can appeciate
Owen Meridith's Lucile
Hope Leslie.

All these here metioned are particular friends &
books that I read all the time & over & over again.

Books & Authors that I hate.—

*Disraeli.*—contemptable
The Newcomes.—(I never could finish)
Guy Livingstone, & all that genre.
Shelley, generally.
Lady Blessington.
Bulwer. detestable style.
Mrs Marsh.
Trollope.
Nearly all Victor Hugos.
Mrs Browning.
Mrs Braddon.—

### MONDAY SEPT 24TH 1871
### PARIS HOTEL WESTMINSTER

FROM Hombourg we went to Mayence, & next day
up the Rhine; deprive it of its castles & I dont think
much would be said about it.—I was charmed with
Cologne, & the Cathedral, three kings, gilded tombs,
jewels & all. It rained the day we were at Brussels
& then we came here.  - -  How much trash is talked,
& enthusism wasted on travelling, when it is the
greatest bore under the sun.—And every one pre-
tends to like it, because they think it is a swell thing
to travel in Europe.—Here we are in this everlasting Paris, & if it were not for the ruins, very pal-

pable witnesses it would be hard to believe in the events of the last year.—All the shopkeepers & workwomen are alive and fat, notwithstanding their horse flesh & patés au rats. I for my part am a staunch Bonapartist, & I hope the Prince Imperial may be Emperor yet.—The hotel de ville is the most picturesque ruin, but the Tuilleries are dismal. —I wonder if people are generally as unquiet & restless at my age as I am.—I am not in the least tranquil or settled.—And then I have read about the boyancy of youth, & how sweet seventeen is supposed to consider life as all couleur de rose.—I dont for one, & I think life is a very small part of existance. —I expect to have plenty of trouble, sorrow, sickness, disappointed hopes & vanished illusions.—But I think Miss Proctor is an angel when she says,

> One by one, thy griefs shall wait thee
> Do not fear an arméd band,
> One will fade as others greet thee
> Shadows passing through the land,
>
> Do not look at lifes long sorrow,
> See how small each moments pain,
> God will help thee for tomorrow
> So each day begin again.

I wish I had a good fat stolid temperament, I believe such people have the easiest time. They sit

through life with folded hands, & dont bother about
any thing.—I dont believe that I shall ever be in
love! First because I do not believe that every one
is capable of feeling a high, pure, disinterested affection. I believe a certain number of people are
capable of feeling it; that a small number *do* feel
it, & that a very very small number of people are
loved in return in an equal degree.—Therefor as
the number is so exceedingly small, it is highly improbable that I shall be an exception to the general
rule.—I believe that true love is founded on mutual
esteem, confidence, similarity of tastes & strong
sympathies. It is certainly the only kind that can
last! I believe that if a girl can feel all this for an
honorable upright, God-fearing man, she should
marry him, & that whether the rest of her life be
happy or unhappy, she will never have to wish herself unmarried. But I think it is better for any one
to scrub floors, than to marry for any other motive.
—I dont think I am capable of feeling a very violent
affection for anyone; it must be very disagreeable
to be in such a state, for if disappointed you are
very miserable, & if all goes well you may be disappointed in the person.—Therefore I hope I may
never feel it!—As for constancy I'm afraid there
is very little in the world; for as nearly all widows
& widowers marry again, it is not to be supposed that

people who have never been united are more faith-ful.—I have been sitting by the window looking out on the "rue de la paix" & I have seen Hamilton Fish, Wittie Crosbie, Mason, H. Hammersly, Suares, & finally I caught sight of Mr Little. I did my best, but he did not go home with the ship, but is here instead with three months leave.—I have seen him several times walking solemly along the side walk, & have passed him on the Champs Elysees almost under his nose, & the goose has n't seen me.—As usual it rains all the time, pour pour, how I hate this place, I am always wretched here. One is always sick or there is something disagreeable.—

TEUSDAY OCT. 2

I wish Mr Little had gone to America, if he only had, if he only had! It would have been all right then, & if after a year or two we had met again, we would have been as good friends as ever. But he is here, & I see him go by the hotel every day, & he never even looks up. People that meddle always spoil everything, & his Mother has done it all; if she hadn't interfered all would have gone right, & there never would have been a bit of trouble. She promised Sister that she would never let him know that she knew about the letter, & now I know she must have told him the whole conversation, or he would have been here. He must have been dreadfully angry, & indeed he has a good right to be; how could she betray his confidence. And then he is such a perfect gentleman it would not have needed much to make him understand, & Sister had no right to tell Mrs Little that "we did not wish to have another Hammersly affair. And we such friends, & I liked him so much; & if they had left us alone he would always have been my friend, always.—And he must feel dreadfully hurt, or he would have come at least to make a formal call if nothing more. If he was an ordinary young man I wouldn't care; but his is a most lovely character, & he is so modest & unpresuming; he never put himself forward, & there was no necessity for any disagreeable feeling, the smallest hint would have been sufficient for him. It is perfectly abominable!

### TEUSDAY OCT. 10

SUNDAY I went to call on Annie Zborowska, No 1 Ave. belle respirot. I found them in a lovely apartement; when I started to go, they insisted on my remaining to dinner, & as I wanted some distraction I stayed.—I was astonished to find what a great invalid Marie Hewith is, though she is large & shows no trace of illness. But Annie told me that she is a martyr to neuraliga headaches of the most fearful kind, added to pains in her spine.—And yet she

keeps up through it all though it has been going on
for four years; besides which she has suffered fearfully from the trial of remedies which have done
no good. She must be one of those wonderful people
who can bear physical pain with a kind of Spartan
firmness, & it is a faculty that I admire beyond anything else. Marie is very handsome in a peculiar
style. A classicaly shaped head, (always a great
beauty,) around which her hair is arranged in a
complicated but artistic manner. Large black eyes,
& good but rather heavily moulded features; the
outlines of her face, neck, arms, & bust are really
splendid; & she looked more like an old picture of
a French woman of the last centuary, than anything
else. But it is alltogether rather a coarse "type", &
she is too mature for a girl of seventeen.—Mrs
Zborowska is a Southern woman by birth, with delicate features & black hair. A woman who can make
herself immensely agreeable when she chooses, &
yet who one feels is never quite sincere. A person
such as you read of in novels, mysterious & irritat-
ing, & yet one that piques curiosity; but I am quite
sure I never would trust her. Annie was the same as
ever, if changed in any way rather toned down &
subdued. She has one of those characters which is
entirely moulded by circumstances & the people she
is thrown with. If she were to live with pious people

she would be pious, & if she lived with fast people she would be fast. I cant understand such people they have no stamina whatever, & are as unfit to take care of themselves as so many babies. Minnie Clapp is just so, I could do anything with, or make anything of that girl that I choose.—I went to the American church the first Sunday after we came; the service was half over when I heard a step in the aisle, & out of the corner of my eye, I saw the skeleton form of J. Hooker Hammesly, sink into a seat directly on a line with Sister.—There he sat, singing psalms cheerily, as though the girl that had refused him were not within three feet of where he sat.— So the world goes so the stream flows, & when the service was over we shook hands as though nothing had ever happened. He blushed most tremendously when he spoke to Sister, & talked faster & louder than ever which was the only sign of his embarrassment. Poor youth his Summer campaigne has been stale, flat, & unprofitable, how he must wish that he had never left his native land.—To day we passed Stouty in a cab, grizzeled & mounful as usual; & yesterday I saw Piquee doing the devoted, the pathetic, & the sentimental, in a salmon colored overcoat, to a young widow. It is not a little curious that four of Sister's & my departed lovers should be here at the same time, & successively promenade before our windows in the rue de la paix. We have so many romantic episodes, that I often prepare myself in the morning, for something that will surely turn up be fore night. I wonder if I shall ever settle down to a quiet humdrum life in one place, & look back with regret on these days.—

OCTOBER 11TH

YESTERDAY morning Mamma & I drove to Pingat's, & ordered the last of my new series of gowns, after which we went up the rue de Rivoli. The street was crowded, & just at a crossing, within ten feet of us was Mr Little. He looked up & caught sight of me, looked down, & then I bowed & he took of his hat, I smiled & so did he in spite of himself, & that is all the communication that has passed between us since he wrote that letter. I have seen him so constantly now for a whole year, that to see him is the most natural thing in the world, & not to speak to him the most unatural.—Sister met Mrs Little the other day, they had quite a chat, & Sister says she was as aimiable as ever. He must have mixed motives for staying away; & I am puzzeled to know what he thinks about it himself.—Of course if he likes me well enough to wish to marry me, he must want to see me, & he can not be angry againts me personally, for it was not I that talked to his Mother. I think he is to young in one way, & to unacustomed

to such things to understand why I acted as I did.
When some other girl has first encouraged & then
snubbed him, he will appreciate it.—

## OCTOBER 13

I AM perfectly bewildered with the rush of events,
I dont know what to write or what to think. Half of
Chicago is in ashes, it is too awful to believe, to
dreadful to think about. And the suspense is so
fearful, the reports so vague & no one can get direct
information. Mr McCagg & seven or eight other
Chicago men are here, the fire began Sunday night,
here it is Friday & we know nothing. I havn't a doubt
the stores on Kinzie street are gone, but I cant & wont
imagine our house is burnt. But oh the misery of the
people, & the destitution of the poor, the sick people
& the little babies. And all the people who are just
comfortably off, & have lost their all. The immediate
destitution is bad enough but the wearing, saving,
pinching years that will come to so many are worse.
We may lose a very great deal, but Papa once said
that if the entire city were to burn down, we should
still have enough to live on. I am so thankful that he
was saved the knowledge of this awful fire, & the
destruction of the city he was so proud of, it would
have embittered all the last days of his life. This
state of suspense is perfectly dreadful; & I have

begun to run down again, as fast as possible. My head is as heavy as lead, & I am so nervous & wretched that I dont know what to do.

### TEUSDAY OCT 17

THE fire began at twelveth street on Sunday night Oct    . It swept the two magnificent avenues, & every building on the South side from twelveth street to the river. The Court House, with the original copy of Father's will & no one knows how many invaluable papers, legal documents, records, the beautiful Crosbie Opera house, a perfect bijoux of a theatre, all the banks, insurance offices, railway depots, churches, & block after block of stores, unequalled any where. And then oh misery, the fire, the red, angry, unrelenting fire, leapt across the river, & burnt & burnt, till Mr Mahlon Ogden's house was the only one left standing up to Lincoln Park. Yes the whole North Side is in ashes, literally in ashes, & every memory connected with my home is gone, every association, every link; never never to be again, irreparably & irrevocably gone.—No one ever loved their home more than I did mine; I loved every angle in the house, every carpet, every table, every picture on the walls, every book in the library, the stairs, the basement, the garret. When the house was rebuilt Papa's room was left untouched, & it was so exactly as it has always been, that his presence seemed to be there; it was sacred, & that is gone! And then my studio, my beautiful studio, & the private staircase, & my room that I have looked forward to furnishing myself in pink & grey.

### THURSDAY OCTOBER 19TH

I SHALL go crazy if I write any more about the fire, —I have felt so bad that I have been in bed for several days, & yesterday afternoon when Mamma & Sister came in, I was lying on the sofa, & feeling as bad as I have ever done since I was first taken sick. —My head felt as if it were filled with molton lead, & it seemed to me as if there was nothing left in the world to live for. I was so wretched that I could not determin how much of my wretchedness was caused by physical weakness, & how much by mental worry & distress.—There was to be a little dance at Annie Zborowska's in the evening to which I had been invited some time previously; we all know by experiance how much good a little excitement occasionally has done me, & so I decided to make a tremendous effort & go, as no matter what happened I could not feel much worse than I did already.—When "Auguste" had dressed my hair, & I was arrayed in a "Worth" gown, I could not help feeling more comfortable, & so away I went. It was a small affair, only

a few girls, & about twenty men, but very jolly nevertheless.—Mrs Zborowska looked like a heathen
godess, & the girls, particularly Annie, betrayed
their seventeen years, by paying more attention to
their gentlemen guests, than to the ladies, when it
was necessary to choose between them.—There was
a Count Dernhoff introduced to me, I did not catch
his name at first, and after a moment he laughed &
said, "mais vous me prenez pour un Français!" Je
suis Allemand!" "Allemand mais pas Prussien?"
Mais oui, Prussien de Berlin même, je suis de la
Legation."—I was so astonished that we both
laughed, & laughed! It was so comical to find myself
talking to an abhorred Prussian; I not only talked
but danced half a dozen times with him, & he waltzed
delightfully.—They got up an impromptu "Cotillon," & he led with Annie & kept asking me out all
the time! My partner was a Monsieur Bixon, a genuine specimin of a Parisian exquiste;—not my style
of man at all, big, broadshouldered masculin, but a
delicately made creature, with soft brown eyes, &
brilliant white teeth under a moustache curled up
at the ends.—

He had that charming manner, which some men
always have towards women, implying that for the
moment you are the one person in the world in
whom they are supremely interested, & a kind of
chivalrous deference which is very taking.—But a

regular Frenchman, false & fickle au fond, I am sure, & amusingly absurd. I told him it was my first cotillon, & so he took it for granted that I was a fresh fledged school-girl, though it puzzled him all along as I could see, as my remarks did not savour particularly of the schoolroom. ——————————

Not a thing was saved from our house not a thing; Mamma's picture, Sister's, my dear little brother Jimmy's, Jamie Clapps & my own painted when I was twelve years old, which Papa was so proud of that he declared there was nothing in the world he would take for it, all were burned to ashes.—Then we have lost all our letters; those of my grand-father, great-grand-father, & even further back, besides those of all my friends, & Sister has lost all of hers; but worse far far worse than all, I have not a morsel left of any of the letters Papa wrote to me; no not one; they were so precious that I did not dare to carry even a few around with me; I had them back to when I was a wee little girl six years old, & I used to write to him, & he to me. I remember one,

My dear Papa,

There was an old man named Grundy, who wipped all his boys every Monday, so all through the week, unable to speak, they only had rest on a Sunday.

Your loving little July

NICE 1861

He took the most extraordinary pains during his long illness to write me the kindest & best letters that ever a Father wrote to his daughter & he kept mine as carefully as I did his; I had them all every one; & now? If I had put them in the safe it would have done no good either for it was burned with the New-berry block; the silver met the same fate in a bank on the South side, & some of it was very pretty. The tea-pot from which Mamma poured the tea, & the china-service beautifully painted which we used on Christmas, the spoons we ate with, & the silver mugs we drank from all are gone. The library too with all Papa's favorite books, that beautiful library in which I expected to spend so many cozy evenings; all my drawings from the beginning at my first water-colors, my monogramme book, & oh misery all my journals that I have taken such pains to write & keep, a record of all my ideas since I first began to have any! My twenty-five dollies poor wretches each roasted in turn, & all my innumerable presents & keepsakes, my beautiful pink bon-bonière with the rest! Mamma lost all her jewelry except her diamond earrings, her cachemere shawls laces, dresses etc. Papa's letters to her; letters from Fenimore Cooper, President Van Buren, Washing-ton Irving, Aaron Burr, (written to Grand Father Clapp,) & quantities of others besides.—But what

is the use of trying to write about it, I have begun
this over & over again & I never can go on beyond
the first few lines.—Who could have dreamed that
when I drove away from the house on that beautiful

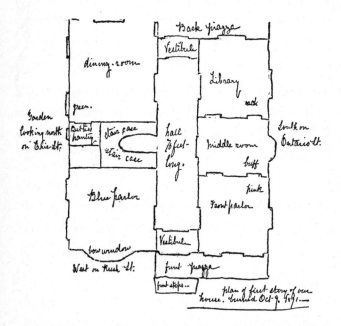

June morning 1870, that I saw it, & all my Chicago
for the last time; if but one or two houses were
burned, but they are all gone, all! It was such a
glorious warm bright day, the trees were so green,
the grass & the flowers; I had left it before so many

times & yet I felt as badly as if it had been the first going away; they all laughed & told me not to waste any sentiment as I should be back in a year or two, & *now*, was my sentiment wasted? The house was so beautiful in itself, & it was home; & now I have no home anywhere; if I had always lived there it would not be so bad, but for years I had looked forward to going back there, & now I have nothing to look forward to.——Papa bought the land, Papa built the house, Papa planted the trees, Papa lived there, & now what is left in the wide world of association with him? nothing; his picture his letters all are burnt away. Why is it so? The last seven months of his life are almost unknown to us, he died far away from us in mid ocean, with no one to care for him when he needed it utterly, no one to learn his last wishes no one to love him; & now with all that the few traces of him are swept away for ever.

### DIED

At Rome, Italy, on the 4th April, 1876, of sudden inflammation of the throat, JULIA ROSA NEWBERRY, only surviving daughter of Julia Butler. and the late Walter L. Newberry.

---

Few announcements will carry more heartfelt sorrow to many friends than the above. With rare personal attractions and unusual artistic and mental gifts, the deceased seemed born to bless and adorn the circle in which she moved. Life's choicest flowers were offered at her feet. Deep sorrow at the loss of her only and much loved sister Mary Louisa, who died in Pau hardly two years since, seriously injured her health, which, it was fondly hoped, varied travel and the warm and equable climate of Egypt had quite restored. The unlooked for and painful experience of a cold and stormy spring in Italy, changed this too happy dream, and it is feared, brought about the sad conclusion. Memory will long retain the sweet images of these two fair sisters : nor can time nor distance fill the void their early deaths have left in the hearts of all who knew them.

FACSIMILE OF NOTICE WRITTEN BY JULIA'S UNCLE WHO HAD JOINED THE FAMILY IN ROME AT THE TIME OF HER DEATH. IT WAS SENT TO JULIA'S FRIENDS AND RELATIVES.

# AFTER WORD

THIS *diary, written by one of my relatives, was found in the summer of
1930. More specifically, the diary itself was opened at that time and read; the book
containing it was familiar to us among a collection of old papers—a book the uninscribed
covers of which were closed by a brass lock to
which the key was missing. A member of the
family chanced across it one rainy Sunday,
stored away in a chest; he broke the lock and
discovered the diary.*

*It came into our possession by the following
succession of events.*

*After the death of her daughters, Mrs. New-
berry stayed abroad, accompanied by her
brother, James Clapp. She died in 1882, leaving to him her Paris apartment, where he continued to live until his death. His will named a
cousin, my father, residuary legatee, and the*

*far-gathered contents of the apartment were shipped across the ocean to our country home in northern New York State. There were in the twenty-eight cases and trunks, together with rugs, Italian madonnas, exotic furniture, things valuable or curious, several box-loads of Mrs. Newberry's papers, forming an apparently complete accumulation of her business and social records, which her brother had left untouched.*

*Our household required many years to absorb this influx of foreign things, and the papers, which were of little interest to us except for the stamps on letters, were consigned to the attic. Long after, my father spent days sorting and destroying most of them. We saved the records and note books, including that of the diary, because by them we could occasionally trace the history of an odd piece of jewelry or china, or the authorship of a painting. There were several locked books and chests, for which we had the proper keys. No key, however, fitted the lock of the diary, but as the task of going through the papers was never quite completed, it was thought the key might appear, and the book was set aside and forgotten and not finally opened until some fifty years after it had probably last been closed.*

*Meanwhile, Julia Newberry was remembered in our household as the subject of a portrait in the hall, an oil painting made in Rome from the photograph used here as the frontispiece; and also as the person to whom had once belonged trunks full of silk dresses and lace petticoats, slippers, dilapidated and quaint finery which two generations of little girls pulled out by candle light from the attic, to costume themselves for plays and games.*

*The form of the book itself completes the charm of its contents. It is a book to tempt a young diarist—particularly a young lady of a diary-writing period. The bindings are of heavy morocco, 6¼ x 9 inches, and between them the gilt-edged leaves were held so tightly by the neat lock that the corners of the pages could not be separated. The publishers are in accord that the script be kept intact in the printed volume, even to the spelling and grammar, so that none of the original character may be lost.*

KATHLEEN KERNAN SLINGLUFF

Baltimore, Maryland

April, 1933